Post-Glacial Communities in the Cambridge Region:

Some Theoretical Approaches to Settlement and Subsistence

Christopher Y. Tilley

B A R British Series 66
1979

B.A.R.

B.A.R., 122 Banbury Road, Oxford OX2 7BP, England

GENERAL EDITORS

A. R. Hands, B.Sc., M.A., D.Phil.
D. R. Walker, M.A.

B.A.R. 66, 1979: " Post-glacial Communities in the Cambridge Region".

ISBN 9780860540533 paperback
ISBN 9781407323374 e-book
DOI https://doi.org/10.30861/9780860540533
A catalogue record for this book is available from the British Library
This book is available at www.barpublishing.com

CONTENTS

LIST OF ILLUSTRATIONS

LIST OF TABLES AND MAPS

PREFACE

In the past decade archaeology has rapidly progressed from a situation of inadequate theory formulation and a virtually non-existent examination of its organizing principles. However there is too little application of archaeological theory to method. The viewing of culture as a system calls for archaeologists to structure their research within a deductive framework, with an orientation toward the generation and testing of models and hypotheses. The restructuring of research strategy does not of itself ensure the attainment of modern archaeological goals. Data collected in the past, upon an inductive basis, is pitifully inadequate to meet the demands of modern archaeological research. Binford (1962) has stated that there are few aspects of sociocultural systems that the archaeologist might not conceivably infer from his peculiar type of raw data. In order to test the assumptions he is making the archaeologist must adopt a problem-orientated approach towards data collection.

This study has been based upon a hypothetico-deductive approach. A number of predictive models are set up concerning settlement and subsistence, as the largely uncontrolled collections of archaeological data that we do have from the region are most amenable to testing the assumptions we make about these particular facets of a sociocultural system. We might argue that these aspects are the most important to be considered as changes in these subsystems may be the primary determinants of the specific form a cultural system takes. To use Steward's (1955) terminology, settlement and subsistence requirements may be viewed as being "core" cultural features.

Flint scatters and a handful of partially excavated sites, along with the distribution of specific tool classes such as tranchet axes, makes up the entirety of the available evidence. This has to bear all the weight of the predictive models, hypotheses and test implications which are erected in this study. The data is, in fact, scarcely adequate to meaningfully lend support or disprove these hypotheses. This situation described for the Cambridge region is by no means exceptional and is the general position in Palaeolithic and Mesolithic research in many areas of Britain and Europe, and the only way to remedy the situation is by means of an intensive programme of field surveys and excavation. Elegant theories must remain sterile unless they can be related to raw data in the real world.

However, theory construction remains of paramount significance in that it provides us with firm guidelines as to what sort of data we should collect and what we may legitimately know, given the constraints of the peculiar type of data with which archaeologists work. The tone of this work is frankly speculative. It should be considered as the first stage in a long-term research programme, a developed body of theoretical assumptions which have yet to be validated concerned with synchronic and temporal changes in the settlement and exploitative patterns of Late-glacial and Mesolithic hunter-gatherer communities in the Cambridge region. The work views such communities from a materialistic perspective and to what extent this conception remains adequate depends, ultimately, on our assumptions and presuppositions about the nature of man: to what extent his activities are ultimately determined by the nature of the environment in which he lives and to what extent he may be considered a 'free agent' in which ideological or other factors are primary, in which case factors of subsistence and settlement may be of only minor importance in an analysis of the mechanisms of societal change (Tilley, 1979).

An attempt is made to use statistical tests to demonstrate the extent to which certain artifact classes tended to cluster in relation to soil types and ecological zones. There certainly does seem to be some geographical trend involved but we lack any independent evidence to test for possible processes. A situation exists where inference is built upon inference and there is nothing but the distribution, which in itself may not mean very much, that is actually tested. In a situation with so little data it is too easy to suggest alternative hypotheses which would fit the scanty evidence equally well.

In view of the large temporal dimension with which we are grappling it might be wise for archaeologists to dispense with the cherished notion of 'site'. A quantitative survey of the density of artifacts across space would, perhaps, be more meaningful. We could, then, go on to equate ecological zones with the frequency of activities involving the various denoted tool kits. This approach would seem to be particularly useful when dealing with largely uncontrolled collections of material, as in this study, which might otherwise have to be excluded from the analysis. In view of the finite nature of our data this would seem to be a particularly important point. A further step in the analysis would be to quantify the presence of artifacts across space using more refined techniques for measuring the ecological productivity of the natural environment (Foley 1977).

As a result of frequent contradictions in national grid references referring to flint scatters and the location of sites, the distribution maps must be considered close approximations rather than true representations of reality. To some extent this will distort the reliability of the significance tests. However, we should heed Cowgill's (1977) words of warning. Significance levels are not statements about the probability of a hypothesis but special kinds of descriptive statements about the sample data which then need to be satisfactorily explained.

No study can be better than the reliability of the theories, observations and analysis upon which it is based. The data we have from the Cambridge region, largely surface collections, can be understood as representing data of a particular kind so that the exercises undertaken are not necessarily invalid, especially as the problem of making comparisons between excavated collections and surface material does not arise to any great degree, although the potential of this data for explaining and explicating socio-cultural change must remain strictly limited.

To my knowledge this is the first systematic attempt to review and interpret the Late-glacial and Mesolithic material within the Cambridge region. It is my hope that this study will promote and encourage future research in this potentially fruitful area. The analysis of the material remains and the compilation of the distribution maps has been as thorough and extensive as possible. All relevant sources of information were consulted in the production of the maps: (i) The records of the Council for British Archaeology's Mesolithic survey of Great Britain (Wymer 1977). (ii) The records of the Ordnance Survey Archaeology Division, Southampton. (iii) The records of the Cambridge Museum of Archaeology and Ethnology. (iv) The results of the M11 Survey. (v) The journals of the Cambridge Antiquarian Society. In addition I have engaged in my own field research including conducting site catchment analyses and looking at material in the possession of local farmers and other collectors. The survey should have accounted for between 80 and 95 per cent of the available data. As will be obvious from the text, the theoretical approach adopted owes much to Jochim's recent book " Hunter-Gatherer Subsistence and Settlement: A Predictive Model" and Clarke's paper "Mesolithic Europe-The Economic Basis?". This study is a revised version of a B.A. dissertation submitted to Cambridge University in May 1977.

ACKNOWLEDGEMENTS

I am indebted to the late Dr. David Clarke for providing the initial encouragement and impetus for this piece of research. I am also indebted to
Dr. Roger Jacobi for his guidance, for providing access to the C.B.A. Mesolithic survey data before the publication of the Gazetteer and for allowing me
to publish several diagrams from his Ph. D. thesis. I would also like to thank
Sir Harry Godwin for allowing me to reproduce his pollen diagrams from Hockham Mere, Dr. John Alexander and Miss Marsha Levine for reading through
and commenting on an earlier version of the text and Dr. Paul Mellars for his
critical comments. Dr. Colin Shell, Miss Mary Craster of the Cambridge
Museum of Archaeology and Ethnology and the Cambridgeshire Archaeology
Officer, Mrs A. Taylor provided me access to information and materials.
Mr. G.W. Clarke of Burwell was particularly helpful in providing access to
his own collection of materials and those of other land owners, showing me
specific sites and allowing me to engage in field walking. Finally I would like
to thank Mr. Paul Archer, Mr. Malcolm Fergusson, Mr. Paul Jefferies and
Mr. David Williams for their support and encouragement. Needless to say,
I alone should be held responsible for all the opinions and interpretations put
forward in this work.

CHAPTER 1

INTRODUCTION

(i) Aims, Procedure and Theoretical Basis

This monograph is an attempt to order and interpret the archaeological evidence for Late and Early Post-glacial societies (10-3,500 b.c.) from a specific region of East Anglia comprising the main drainage basin and watersheds of the Ouse and Cam rivers and their tributaries, Map A .   Binford (1964) has convincingly argued that the region is the analytical unit most appropriate to current archaeological research if we wish to adopt a systematic perspective.   Cultural variations in space represent different adaptive requirements to the natural and social environment.   Since the physical environment is structured we should expect this to be reflected by the settlement network.   Changes in ecological conditions should result in different social configurations and exploitative economies.(Streuver 1968, 1971). Emphasis will be given both to synchronic (functional) and diachronic (evolutionary) models.   The study of change is an almost inevitable outcome of archaeological research and by focussing study on a few theoretical predictive models we can hope to underline the critical variables at work (Plog 1974).

In this study culture is viewed from a systemic perspective, the main principles of which are adequately discussed elsewhere (Binford 1965; Clarke 1968; Flannery 1967; Renfrew 1972).   A system may minimally be defined as an interconnected network of attributes or entities forming a complex whole characterized by continual change and other properties such as feedback, different types of equilibrium and homeostasis, having more characteristics than the sum of its components.   The subsistence and settlement behavioural patterns of a prehistoric community are the result of a set of decisions which attempt to resolve specific, but interrelated, problems.   The identification of these problems will define the boundaries of the system.   The objective guiding the solutions of the problems will provide the goals of the system (Jochim 1976:8).   An ecological perspective is given primary importance within the framework of the systematic analysis as the relationship between man and the biotope is one of the most important factors conditioning economic and social behaviour.   The culture of a human population is regarded as the distinctive means by which a population maintains itself in the ecosystem.   The study will attempt to test a series of models relating to settlement and subsistence within the context of a functioning and changing socio-cultural system. As Clarke (1972a) has emphasized it is the construction, testing, verification or refutation and modification of explicit models that is the essence of the empirical and scientific approach providing the progressive cycle by means of which fresh information and insight are gained, explanations are reached, and theory accumulated.

1

(ii) A Brief History of Past Research

Fox's "Archaeology of the Cambridge Region" (1923) was the first systematic attempt to describe and interpret archaeological material from the region. He did not consider Mesolithic material at all and his discussion of the Neolithic was primarily concerned with providing a background for later developments. He was one of the few archaeologists to realize the value of a regionally based diachronic approach and was a pioneer in this field. At that time so little data was available and the interpretative paradigms so weakly developed that it was possible to do little more than plot the main artifact distributions, outline the main trends and discuss typological developments.

In 1932 the interdisciplinary Fenland Research Committee was founded and carried out work at Shippea Hill, Plantation Farm and other sites. The emphasis of this research was primarily stratigraphic (chronological) and environmental, the then new technique of pollen analysis being applied in order to provide a relative date for archaeological phases. A picture of the changing regional flora could be built up and related to different assemblages. The main research objectives had been completed by 1936 and the committee finally split up with the advent of war in 1940 (Phillips 1951).

Subsequent research in the area was limited to the work of individuals notably Professor J. G. D. Clark who, in an important publication (Clark 1955), analyzed a microlithic industry from Shippea Hill suggesting "Sauveterrian" continental affinities. In 1960 fresh excavations of a limited nature were undertaken at Shippea Hill, in order to provide radiocarbon samples providing an important sequence of dates. In 1972 the only systematic field sampling to have taken place within the region was carried out along a narrow strip marking the proposed position of the M11 motorway. Local enthusiasts and collectors have always been active within the region. Todd in 1947 excavated a Mesolithic occupation on Lackford Heath and the finds are in the British Museum. A number of general reviews of the material have been published since Fox's work (Clark 1938, Clarke, R. R. 1960, Coles 1965) but there has never been any detailed attempt to analyze the data. Chronology, stratigraphy controls and typological analysis have always been given primary importance in these discussions which amount to little more than slotting sites and artifacts into the spatio-temporal boundaries of cultural traditions.

(iii) The nature of the evidence and sampling problems

Only small areas, amounting to little more than test trenches have been investigated on all the sites excavated within the region. This was sufficient for past archaeological paradigms but is manifestly inadequate for those of the present day. We have anything approaching an absolute chronology based upon isotopic dating techniques for only one site, Shippea Hill. Typological analysis provides only broad relative dates for other sites. In view of the rapid advances in excavation technology we must seriously question the reliability of the samples obtained from many of the excavated sites, particularly the minimal recovery of organic remains. There is an almost total lack of faunal data of any description.

2

Other sites which have not been excavated are marked by the presence of surface flint scatters. These are extremely difficult to date or interpret. Surface collections are generally biased towards the more substantial and/or recognizable components of the industries. In many cases it is virtually impossible to distinguish between a Mesolithic and a Neolithic flint assemblage apart from the presence of a few "diagnostic", usually rare and atypical, tool classes. Differential patination as demonstrated by Clark (1955) may help but is by no means an infallible guide. It is not possible to determine the possible nature of the underlying material or delimit site boundaries purely on the evidence of flint scatters because of plough disturbance and other factors. This makes any attempt at arriving at population estimates or other sociological inferences from such data suspect. Many finds, especially those of Mesolithic tranchet axes, were made in the late nineteenth century and provenance is uncertain except within the boundaries of a parish.

To what extent are artifact or site distributions the result of differential preservation, uneven research work, or other factors such as uneven vegetational cover and agricultural activities? The fact that archaeological samples are never randomly deposited, preserved or recovered is an inherent research problem. We can assume that if denudation was generalized over this land area through time it would act approximately randomly in bringing material deposited in the ground to the surface. In any systematic field survey we might hope to gain a random sample of the artifact populations of underlying sites, but in the case of our study area this is, perhaps, wishful thinking. Clarke (1972b:804-807), Schiffer and Rathje (1973) and Schiffer (1976) have argued that it is only through the erection of geomorphological models and the explicit consideration of natural and cultural transformation processes that we can efficiently bridge and gap between the operation of post-cultural systems and the interpretation of data in the archaeological record.

Using an analogy with the Wessex Chalklands (Evans 1975:141) it is suggested that denudation may have been fairly uniform over the chalky boulder clay regions but less so over the chalk escarpment/river terrace areas (Map 1), with the removal of the natural to a depth approaching two feet since the last glaciation. This would act approximately randomly upon the chalky boulder clay plateaux in bringing artifacts and/or settlement locales to the surface. In view of the differential rates of permeability and surface run-off in the chalk/river terrace gravel areas we would expect that distribution of archaeological material might be to a greater extent the product of differential erosion. The Breckland zone of the north-east is characterized by a rapid rate of erosion especially by wind in areas of disturbed ground, in contrast with areas stabilized by plant communities, and this would lead to the differential revelation of archaeological features. The fen basin was, for the entire time period being considered, a major area of alluviation resulting in the burial of archaeological material. The phenomenon of peat wastage since the draining of the Fens has been commented upon by many authors (Fowler 1937, Perrin and Hodge 1965, Taylor 1973), revealing in many areas extinct watercourses or "roddons". The frequent association of prehistoric material with sand deposits has led to the suggestion that these areas were those primarily selected for settlement (Clark 1934; Clarke 1960). This may not necessarily be the case and we may have a badly distorted artifact distribution. In this

3

context it would be unwise to place undue emphasis on negative evidence when considering settlement and subsistence systems.

Most individual finds have been made by local collectors on a random and spasmodic basis. Three separate areas have had differential attention largely owing to their proximity to the homes of interested individuals. (i) The Breckland region of the north-east. (ii) An area of the south-western fen margin around Swaffham Prior and Burwell. (iii) The area near to Duxford in the south-west of the region.

In the absence of any controlled surveys, many of the contrasts in artifact densities and the positions of the sites might be discounted as a result of sampling bias, but the artifact density in relation to soil types and ecological zones would appear to be too large and the locational regularities of the sites too repetitive to be explained entirely in terms of distorting factors resulting from differential deposition and erosion and differences in the intensity of local research.

CHAPTER II

THE CAMBRIDGE REGION

(i) Geology and Topography

The region considered in this monograph covers an area of 2560 km^2, being marginally smaller than the area used by Fox in his 1923 analysis. The actual boundaries were arbitrarily defined for research purposes and as such it cannot be considered a 'natural' region. There are no dramatic differences in relief. The highest ground is in the south-east, reaching approx. 400 ft O.D. General areas above 200 ft, the main towns, drainage and the spatial limits of the region are shown on map A.

A gentle, subdued, chalk escarpment runs across the district diagonally from Royston in the south-west to Icklingham in the north-east. Even where the escarpment is relatively high this may only involve an immediate fall of 50-100 ft. South and East of the escarpment there is no simple dip slope but a rolling till plateau capping a variety of upper Jurassic and lower Cretaceous rocks (Worssam and Taylor 1969). To the west of Cambridge a similar plateau capped with boulder clay reaches a maximum elevation of 270 ft O.D. In the south-west of the region in the front of the chalk escarpment are a series of fragmentary river terraces ranging up to 300 ft O.D. A series of late Pleistocene river terrace deposits are strung along the Cam in the vicinity of Cambridge. Upstream these are replaced by an erosional feature termed the "low plain" (Sparks and West 1965). The broken, hummocky, sandy terrain of Breckland in the north-east of the region with a general elevation of 100-150 ft O.D. is a relic of Pleistocene periglacial conditions. The north is dominated by the fen basin filled with a great series of clay, silt and peat deposits, an area with an elevation only slightly above modern sea level. A number of knolls composed of various solid formations, capped with drift, form the Fen islands. This basic topography has remained little changed since the retreat of the ice sheets at the end of the last glaciation. The topography and geological structure is simple in outline but complex in detail, the juxtaposition of a wide variety of different drift and solid deposits resulting in considerable ecological diversity.

(ii) Climate

The climatic regime can be broadly classified as 'continental' with a summer rainfall maximum of 2.16 in. during July as compared with 1.50 in. in January (Watt 1938). The rainfall is characteristically low, the average for twenty-eight stations within Cambridgeshire being 22.5 in. Annual evaporation is approximately 17 in. which leaves 5-7 in. for ground water recharge and surface run-off. The region is one of the driest areas of Britain and in many areas water deficiency remains a perennial problem, especially in areas such as Breckland with porous soils. The mean January temperature is 4 ^{o}C and that for July 18°C. Even minor differences in topography may be significant as a few feet may raise an area above the accumulation of cold air or fog and this may be a critical factor in settlement location.

(iii) Drainage

The drainage pattern shown on the distribution maps is adopted from Fox (1923) and is an attempt to reconstruct the pre-fen-drainage system from historical and geological sources. The courses of the fen rivers were, no doubt, frequently altered in prehistoric as in historic times. The fenland is an area of substantial deposition prone to seasonal flooding. Concomitants of this are the development of temporary and permanent lakes, shifting sandbanks and braided river channel systems.

(iv) Soils

Soils have been extensively studied within the region (Hodge and Seale 1966). For the purposes of this paper four basic types deemed to be of arch-aeological significance will be distinguished (Map B).

(i) Brown earth/Rendzina soils derived from the sands and gravels of river terrace deposits and the chalk escarpment. These are friable, free draining, and have a high agricultural potential; 815 km^2.

(ii) The basin peat soils which would be naturally waterlogged; 607 km^2.

(iii) Breckland soils. These are sandy with a limited humus content, locally heavily podzolized with very free drainage; 165 km^2.

(iv) Heavy clay soils developing upon the chalky boulder clay plateaux with imperfect, locally waterlogged, drainage; 973 km^2.

(v) Ecological zonation.

At a general level we can divide the natural vegetation which once existed in the region into four major classes, broadly correlating with the soil type zones (Map C).

(i) "Damp" deciduous forest, subdivided into two areas: (a) on the boulder clay plateaux and on river terrace gravels; 1555 km^2, and (b) on the chalk escarpment; 135 km^2.

(ii) "Dry" deciduous forest on the Breckland soils; 116 km^2.

(iii) Fen vegetation; 460 km^2.

(iv) The fen edge/deciduous forest ecotone; 294 km^2, an area approx. 3 miles wide.

A discussion of these postulated ecological zones and their resource potentials follows below (Chapter IV, section iv).

CHAPTER III

LATE-GLACIAL SUBSISTENCE AND SETTLEMENT:
10,000-8,500 b.c.

(i) The Material Culture

British Late-glacial industries exhibit a unique combination of stone and antler tool classes, most of which have precise European parallels but are unknown elsewhere in combination (Campbell 1977:197; Jacobi 1976). The flint industry is characterized by a predominance of backed tools and includes backed and truncated blades, and scrapers, steeply retouched awls, points, burins and uniserially or biserially barbed antler points with round to sub-oval stems (Mellars 1974:71-74).

(ii) The Environment

Around 10,500 b.c. it is likely that the mean July temperature was close to 13-14°C. At Church Stretton, Shropshire, a highly thermophilous Coleopeteran fauna of pollen zone I was replaced close to the opening of zone II by one representative of colder conditions and this is dated to 10,185 ± 200 b.c. Winter temperatures would have remained well below freezing (Osborne 1971: 351). The general period under consideration represents the recessional stage of the last glaciation. The climate did not really begin to steadily ameliorate until towards the end of zone III when the ice sheets had already begun to retreat towards the north. Temperatures during this 'Allerød' interstadial were evidently just warm enough to permit the migration of scattered birch woodland into many parts of south-east England. The evidence from the insect faunas indicate earlier dates for the worsening of the climate during zone II than the botanical evidence and this may be related to their more rapid response to environmental change. The end of the Allerød interstadial was marked by a return to essentially arctic conditions during the 'Younger Dryas' phase. The end of the Late-glacial period is marked by an increase in temperatures which is represented in the pollen diagrams by the establishment of a well developed forest cover over most areas of England.

Pollen diagrams from East Anglia (Figs. 1-4) are indicative of lightly wooded conditions within the region being considered. At Hockham Mere, Norfolk, tree pollen varies between 60 and 80% of the sample analyzed (DB5, Fig. 1). Birch dominates (70-90%) with pine (10-15%) and willow during zone II. Grasses, herbs and ferns indicate substantial areas of relatively open ground cover.

In zone III at Hockham Mere (Godwin and Tallantire 1951) tree pollen fluctuates between 20 and 70%. Birch still dominates but pine is becoming increasingly important (20-40%) and willow attains values between 10 and 20%. Pinus may be over-represented in the pollen diagrams as a result of its high pollen productivity coupled with wind dispersal (Godwin 1975:49).

Within the Cambridge region we should expect (i) a comparatively light birch-pine forest development on the light sandy Breckland soils of the north-east, (ii) perhaps a denser vegetation cover on the boulder clay plateaux, along river terraces and on the chalk escarpment dominated by Betula with Salix locally important along river valleys and in waterlogged areas and (iii) immature oligotrophic lakes with low nutrient concentrations forming in depressions left by the ice sheets, fringed with water loving plant communities. Most surface water would remain permanently frozen between September and May.

At this time a light woodland zone may have extended along the entire east coast of England (Campbell 1977:351), while other areas were more or less open tundra with a combination of Alpine, steppe and Arctic plants which Clarke (1976) has aptly described as a "photosynthetic desert" (Clarke 1976: 450). Consequently animal foodstuffs would have been of primary importance.

(iii)   Resource use schedule and settlement location

The ecosystem which had developed in the Cambridge region was still relatively specialised with a low plant/animal species diversity index and its potentiality for supporting human populations was, therefore, limited. The birch/pine forest would have an estimated number of 100-200 edible species of plants with a net primary productivity of 400-2,000 g/m^2/year (Phillipson 1966; Whittaker 1970:83; Clarke 1976:464). Coniferous forests provide poor environments for ungulates which are only able to attain comparatively low population densities (Taber 1963:207; Webb 1960:149-50). Possibilities of plant exploitation which would be significant in calorific terms were probably limited to edible roots, berries and leaves with autumn perhaps being the primary exploitation season. The lakeside vegetative communities would have been of greatest significance during the warmer summer months when the starch-rich rhizomes of the lakeside plant communities may have been a particularly important food source.

The main animal populations inhabiting the region would have been (i) migratory herds of reindeer, (ii) horse, (iii) bos/bison, (iv) beaver, (v) elk and (vi) small game such as arctic fox and wolf (cf. Campbell 1977:Vol. II, Table 31, p. 69). Jacobi (1976) has proposed a general economic model for Britain with regard to reindeer exploitation during this period. He envisaged seasonal herd movement from the taiga ecotone of areas such as the Cambridge region to what he postulates may have been the summer parturition grounds in mountainous districts such as Wales and the Pennines. We should expect, therefore, that reindeer would only be important between October and April in the Cambridge region. Horse and bos/bison may have been present all the year round but as an economic resource would have been especially important during the summer months because of the absence of reindeer. Also we might expect them to group together in larger aggregations at this season due to the greater availability of browse. We might expect their preferred grazing areas to have been on the birch/pine-fen basin ecotone as this is our richest hypothetical resource zone, on ecological grounds. Beaver would have been of maximum importance during the winter months due to their aggregation in lodges with limited mobility. Small game, fish and wildfowl exploitation may have been of primary importance in the fen basin during the summer. Fig. 5 represents this hypothetical resource use schedule for Late-glacial communities in the Cambridge region in diagrammatic form.

We can distinguish from this hypothetical picture of resource use two main economic seasons alternating between two exploitation regions of maximum importance: the Breckland region to the north-east and the Fen basin. In autumn and winter reindeer may have been the main food source. Jacobi (1976) has emphasized the lack of predictability of such a mobile resource. Most animals may have been killed in a relatively short time period, maybe a few days to a month, as has been suggested for the Meindorf/Stellmoor continental Late-glacial sites (Clark 1975:90), during which time the herds would move in their migratory cycle along well-defined migration routes. As we have seen, this may have been from highland summer parturition grounds to overwintering areas in the birch/pine forests. Campbell (1977: 159, 176) postulates that the East Anglian sites may represent primarily spring and autumn occupation sites, with the implicit and unsupported assumption that the human populations moved away in the summer.

In autumn and spring we might expect sites to be so positioned along the predicted movement paths of the reindeer. During the winter, after the autumnal kill, it would be possible to cache meat supplies in the frozen subsoil for future use. On ecological grounds we can argue that it would be to the Breckland area of the Cambridge region that the herds of reindeer would move due to the light woodland cover on the poor sandy soils where there would be a greater availability of browse. Exploitation of the reindeer herds in the winter would be more difficult and not very efficient as the animals, once they had reached their overwintering areas, would be much more dispersed than during their seasonal movements.

In autumn and spring[1] we might expect the human populations to aggregate in a few large kill sites while in winter and summer they might disperse into smaller social units. In winter, settlements situated near to the oligotrophic lakes of the fen basin might exploit beaver, rich in fats and protein. In spring the population might aggregate, returning to formerly occupied kill sites in order to exploit the migrating herds. In summer the fen basin may have been the most favourable region in terms of resource potential due to its wide fish, wildfowl, and plant resources. The latter would attract horse and bison/bos to the area.

The economic analysis has rested upon the assumption that the Cambridge region was habitually occupied by at least one or more social groups utilizing a series of complementary sites within an economic system tightly based on seasonality and scheduling (Flannery 1968). Sturdy (1975:75-8), Clark (1975: 89) and other authors have suggested that Late-glacial human groups would have been nomadic, exploiting the migratory reindeer herds upon which their economy was largely based. It is the contention here that such an exploitation system is unlikely in view of the large distances involved, the speed and lack of predictability of herd movement and the availability of more stable food resources in the Cambridge region all the year round.

9

(iv) An analysis of the evidence in relation to the proposed economic model

In the Cambridge region we have three sites attributable to this period:
(i) Whiteway Drove, Swaffam Prior; (ii) Mildenhall Fen; and (iii) London
Bottom, Icklingham. The Royston bone point, whose exact provenance is
uncertain, may also belong to this period. Campbell (1977) does not mention
the Swaffham site and considers that only the London Bottom site may belong
to this period.

Fig. 6 represents an analysis of the flint industry from the Swaffam Prior
site. Scrapers, burins and spalls from tool manufacture are the most numerous tool classes. There are comparatively few backed, truncated or retouched blades or penknife points which might be interpreted as components
of projectiles. This is what we would expect if we were dealing with a generalized assemblage representing a number of integrated activities. The tool
kit contrasts markely with the limited numbers of rather specialized tools,
probably associated with reindeer hunting, that are a feature of some of the
Pennine cave sites (Jacobi 1976). The hypothesis put forward here is that
the Swaffam site represents a summer or mid-winter settlement on the basis
of our economic model and the rather generalized nature of the assemblage
would seem to confirm this view. Faunal evidence is lacking so that there
can be no more conclusive evidence as regards seasonality. As the lithic
material is derived from surface collections we might expect a bias toward
heavy processing tools associated with animal resources, hide scrapers,
burins and large blades, while perhaps the less distinctive tools utilized in plant
food collecting and processing might not be recognized in either the analysis
or the surface collections. The site catchment analysis (Fig. 7) (for a summary
of principles see Jarman 1972b) suggests that the settlement was located on
the margins of the fen basin, perhaps being orientated towards the exploitation
of the lightly wooded areas of the chalk escarpment to the east and plant and
other food resources such as beaver associated with the oligotrophic lake
ecology of some areas of the fen basin to the north, west and south.

The Mildenhall Fen site, the exact provenance of which is uncertain, being
located somewhere in the Wangford/Mildenhall area of the east of the Cambridge
region, produced a large series of shouldered points and backed tools but the
collections are mixed and have never undergone any systematic analysis.
Campbell (1977:140) mentions surface finds from this general area which
almost certainly belong to this assemblage. The materials are in the British
Museum (labelled 'Fenton collection') (Jacobi, personal communication).

The London Bottom site (Campbell 1977:176) is located adjacent to a river
valley in an area which probably supported a light cover of birch/pine woodland
(Fig. 8), The settlement is located on what was very probably a migration
route for reindeer herds, which we might expect to follow the main river valleys such as the Lark (Map A) in order to reach their overwintering areas in
the Breckland area to the east of the Cambridge region, which with its dry
sandy soils and light woodland cover may have been a particularly favourable
area for reindeer during the winter.

The London Bottom assemblage is mixed with Mesolithic and later artifacts but includes 8 large convex backed blades, two large 'Cheddar' points,
burins and blade end scrapers (Campbell 1977:176). The evidence from this

site and that from the nearby Mildenhall/Wangford area is obviously too scanty to test for seasonality or economic strategy, but, at least, does not conflict with our economic model and provides us with some guidelines as to likely settlement locations which could be used to direct future research.

CHAPTER IV

THE MESOLITHIC PERIOD; SUBSISTENCE AND SETTLEMENT
8, 500-3, 500 b. c.

(i) The implications of environmental change

The economic impact of the change from Late-glacial to Post-glacial
conditions has been stressed by many authors (Butzer 1972:577; Clark 1936:
29-30; Clark 1968; 1975:99). Clark (1968) states that "in particular the
Late-glacial hunters were confronted by a drastic crisis.....when the reindeer
herds disappeared" (Clark 1968:243). This has been interpreted in terms of
a drastic reduction in biomass with the resultant need for an "intensification
of the food quest" (ibid.), with the need to utilize a far wider range of resources.
A possible concomitant of this was the reduced optimum size for the social
group. The contrary viewpoint is argued here. The disappearance of migratory reindeer herds from Britain and their replacement by a less gregarious,
but more stable, woodland fauna, coupled with the growing affects of climatic
amelioration upon the natural vegetation represents a great improvement in
resource potential and may have led to significant increases in population
density. There may have been no site territory without ungulate or plant
resources of some sort at any time of the year contrasting with the dearth or
seasonal abundance experienced by late glacial populations (Jacobi 1976).
Assuming Leibig's law of the minimum, population densities always had to be
adjusted to the latter possibility. The general trend during the Mesolithic
is toward an increasing number of potential subsistence strategies. any one
of which or several in combination could be selected from a wide range of
alternatives. The edible potentiality of any region is likely to be perceived
within the bounds of a particular cognitive framework by any one group of
hunter-gatherers so that the validity of modern ecological calorific estimates
of potential carrying capacity may be seriously questioned. For example,
of the 223 local species of animals known and named by the !Kung Bushmen,
54 are classified as edible. and of these, only 17 species were hunted on a
regular basis. Although 85 species of edible plants are known, only 23 species
contribute 90 per cent of the vegetable diet by weight (Lee 1968). During the
later part of the Mesolithic, when environmental conditions reached an optimum
level, we have growing evidence for the development of predetermined subsistence arrangements which could be carried out by means of the manipulation
of plant and animal food resources.

(ii) The material culture

The flint industries may be divided into two broad chronological phases.
Between 8, 500 and 6, 800 b. c. the microlithic industries are dominated by
"wide" forms - obliquely blunted points with or without a smaller proportion
of wide isosceles triangles, elongated trapezes and points with convex blunting

13

down one side. "Narrow" microlithic forms are absent (Jacobi 1973; Mellars 1974). This material is that formerly referred to as "Maglemosian" (Clark 1936, 1955). After 6,800 b.c. flint industries exhibit a wide range of "narrow" forms - blades with straight retouch along one edge, micro-crescents, rhomboids and hollow-based points. This typological sequence is validated stratigraphically at Lackford Heath. The later industries are those described by Clark (1955) as having "Sauveterrian" affinities. Some of the earlier forms persist in the later industries at sites such as Lakenheath, Wangford and Shippea Hill, indicating technological and, we can infer, social continuity. Heavy core tools, notably transversely sharpened flint axes, can occur in both the earlier and the later industries.

The specific functional interpretation of the various microlith forms is notoriously difficult. The usual inference is that they represent the tips and barbs of wooden arrows and that the earlier and later types were utilized in projectile heads of a different form (Mellars 1976a:396). However, Clarke (1976:453-456) suggests that a more important and possibly primary use may be related to vegetable food processing activities. There appears to be little reason to adopt any exclusive hypothesis for microlith function. Their high degree of standardization would fit them for a wide variety of uses. White and Thomas (1972) demonstrate how many typological distinctions that arch-aeologists make are largely irrelevant as to how tools are actually utilized by aboriginal populations. Clarke (1976:467) discusses the considerable tech-nological sophistication of microlithic flint technology. This technique enables the maximum length of cutting edge and points to be extracted from a minimal flint volume as a result of the use of composite tools with a flint armature that was rapidly interchangeable due to unit standardization.

(iii) The Environment

The period is that of pollen zones IV-VIIa, embracing the prisere (suc-cessional development) of the Pre-boreal, Boreal and Atlantic phases. The pollen diagram from Hockham Mere in zone IV (Pre-boreal) (Figs. 1-4) shows a forest still dominated by birch and pine but with a significant decline in non-tree pollen, perhaps indicating a denser tree cover with fewer open areas than had existed previously. Birch begins to decline in frequency at the begin-ning of zone V (Boreal), accounting for only c. 50% of the tree pollen by the end of this period. Pine exhibits a significant increase. Hazel increased dramatically and this would indicate large areas of hazel scrub. This is gen-erally thought to be a climatic effect or to be due to the migration rate of hazel outstripping that of other thermophilous trees (Godwin 1956:200). Throughout zone VI birch maintains low values at Hockham and in the pollen diagrams for Shippea Hill (Godwin 1934, 1960). Pine remains an important element of the forest until subzone VIc where it exhibits a rapid decline. Deciduous trees (elm and oak) first begin to colonize the area in subzone VIa and become dominant in subzone VIc in which the highly thermophilous lime and alder first appear. The latter is indicative of the west conditions pre-vailing around the lakeside at Hockham Mere and along the fen edge at Shippea Hill. Hazel maintains high values throughout zone VI at Hockham and at Shippea Hill but appears to decline in zone VIc. At Shippea Hill this decline occurs at the time of the Mesolithic occupation in zone VIc. Godwin (1975:32) has noted a phase of dryness at the end of pollen zone VI which reduced lake levels at Hockham. If this was associated with burning and/or land clearance this could account for the hazel decline at Shippea Hill.

Throughout zones V and VI the climate was gradually ameliorating, hence the continuous vegetative instability exhibited in the pollen record. Pioneer species such as birch were replaced by hazel, which is in turn replaced by a mixed deciduous forest. The Atlantic period by contrast, zone VIIa, is one of ecological stability with a mixed lime-oak-elm-hazel-deciduous forest dominating the landscape, being the climax vegetation at this latitude and lime and oak being co-dominants (Birks et al. 1975; Godwin 1975:59-61). Temperatures were probably 2-3°C warmer than those prevailing today and rainfall may have been slightly greater. The general vegetative trend is one of increasing diversity leading to the development of a complex, generalized ecosystem. The lake and river system in the fen basin gradually matured from an oligotrophic state (poor in nutrients) prior to 8,500 b.c. to become fully eutrophic or mature during the Atlantic period. The meres would have become shallower with a far greater primary productivity with a dense plankton population and abundant littoral vegetation.

(iv) Resource use schedule-plant foods

Jochim's (1976) study demonstrates the possibility of being able to predict both resource utilization patterns and the derivation of economic seasons independently from direct archaeological evidence from studies of animal ecology and ethology and edible plant productivity. Jochim estimates resource weight, density, aggregation size, mobility and non food yields (hides, furs, bone for tool manufacture etc.) and uses these to predict the proportional utilization of various food sources on a monthly basis for prehistoric populations during different seasons of the year. The model was applied to an ethnographically documented group, the round lake Ojibwa living in northern Ontario, and to Mesolithic material from south-west Germany. Two primary goals are assumed to govern the relative seasonal utilization of resources: (a) the provision of food, a basic biological requirement, along with non-food products, and (b) energy minimization in the procurement of these resources. A non-quantitative use of this general model is employed here. An additional assumption stimulated by Clarke's (1976) seminal paper is that plant food may have made a far more significant contribution to the total diet than has been previously recognized. Hunting is far more problematic than food collecting, being a high yield, high risk strategy. Some indication of this may be seen from Noe-Nygaard's (1974) investigation of fractured animal bone from the Danish and North German Mesolithic, with a ratio of 0.7 healed/unhealed fractures for the Boreal and 1.8 for the Atlantic and Sub-boreal periods. This indicates that far more animals may have escaped their human predators than those that were successfully killed.

We should expect that plant foods would become progressively more important and the ecosystem more diversified throughout the period that is being considered. For the mixed coniferous and deciduous Pre-boreal and Boreal forest, we can estimate that the proportion of edible plants would be quite high. Clarke (1976) cites figures of 200-350 species. The net primary productivity may have been about 400-2,000 g/m^2/annum. During the late Boreal and Atlantic periods the number of edible species may have been greater (250-400) and net primary productivity may have risen to around 600-3,000 g/m^2/annum (Whittaker 1970:83). We would expect that the distribution, territories and annual subsistence strategies of Mesolithic communities would be closely related to the primary edible productivity of the various ecological communities existing within the Cambridge region and the efficiency with which the successively productive areas could be integrated within an annual circuit. Plants may have been the most abundant and reliable primary food resources. Clarke (1976) makes the important point that many natural ecosystems have a greater edible productivity than many agricultural systems with a "full photosynthetically active plant cover throughout the year trapping sunlight in complex layers of mutually adjusted foliage and roots" (1976:467).

Deciduous Forest

The mixed deciduous forest of the Atlantic climatic optimum was characterized by a complex internal structure. In contemporary deciduous forests a number of different layers may be distinguished: (i) a tree layer, (ii) a shrub layer, (iii) a herb or field layer, and (iv) the ground layer (Tansley 1965:276). In each stratum one or more species dominates. Competition within and between species is constant. In the Atlantic climatic communities this may have kept the composition of the population and the structure of the community in a stable state, that is in equilibrium. As there is virtually no natural deciduous forest left in Europe it is very difficult to obtain an accurate impression of the diversity and abundance during the Atlantic. Some indication of the nature of the Atlantic forest is provided by the 'bog oaks' dug out from the fens which are typically very straight with little lateral branching and up to 27 m in length, indicative of a forest structure far more massive than contemporary examples with severe competition for light so that any laterial branches would soon wither and die. In the one largely natural area of European deciduous forest still remaining, at Biatistok in eastern Poland, the forest trees, lime and oak being dominant, reach heights of 36.5 m with short crowns and trunks with few lateral branches (Godwin 1978:37).

Subsidiary trees form the shrub layer, becoming particularly prolific in forest edge or glade situations, the main species being hazel (usually dominant) with crab apple, wild cherry, juniper, hawthorn, blackthorn, blackberry and rowan, all providing valuable sources of fruits, nuts and berries, many of which would have had considerable potential for storage if processed in the correct manner. The local dominants of the field layer would be bracken and societies of gregarious herbs and flowers blooming profusely in early spring, the bulbs, roots, rhizomes, tubers and flowers of which could be collected and consumed relatively easily. The ground layer would have been dominated by edible lichens, mosses, grasses, liverworts and fungi among a thick layer of decomposing leaf litter.

The structure of the entire deciduous forest is based on autumnal leaf loss and the cessation of growth for three to five months of the year. A minutely integrated schedule of leaf loss, flowering and fruiting is correlated with light intensity and the degree of shade, ensuring an abundance of foodstuffs at most seasons. The detailed structure of the forest can be spatially related to dampness and the acidity of the underlying soils (Tansley 1965:271-272), producing considerable local horizontal diversity. Tansley draws a basic distinction between 'damp' and 'dry' types of deciduous forest. 'Damp' forests are characteristic of clay and loam soils while 'dry' forests exist on coarser sandy soils. The 'damp' forest may be differentiated from the 'dry' forest on the basis of a richer floristic composition in the former which also contrasts in having a much denser understorey shrub vegetation (Tansley 1965:271, 286-7). On the boulder clay plateaux and on areas of alluvium and river terrace gravels within the Cambridge region we would expect to find predominantly 'damp' deciduous forest with rich and abundant field and shrub layers with a high diversity index. Place-name evidence (Rackham 1976: 55-57) lends some support to this supposition because 'damp' deciduous forest areas would be particularly difficult to clear and might well survive into historical times, while the 'dry' deciduous forest may have been the first to have been cleared (see below). Village names ending in 'ley' or 'leigh', derived from the Anglo-Saxon lēah, meaning a glade or a clearing in the 'wildwood', imply that some of this wildwood remained when these villages were built. Such village or hamlet names cluster in the west of the Cambridge region and on the Suffolk border in the south-east being concentrated in areas on boulder clay.

On the light, dry and acid sands of the Breckland area in the north-east we would expect to find a more open, less diversified, vegetative community with hazel and bracken predominant in the shrub and field layers respectively (Tansley 1965:279-280). The combination of these two resources might be especially important in the autumn as a result of their high productivity per unit area. Hedrick (1972:470) has described the use of bracken-like ferns as one of the primary staples of the pre-contact Maori economy, and documented evidence for its use as a substitute for bread in Europe in the seventeenth and eighteenth centuries.[2] Clarke (1976:475) cites figures of 20-50 tonnes of edible bracken root/km^2. Jacobi (1978a:82-3) suggests the possibility that hazel nuts may have provided 25% of the total diet for four months of the year. Ethnographic accounts of the importance of mongongo nuts to the !Kung Bushmen economy lend credibility to these arguments (Lee 1968: 34, 39). Oak trees may yield 700-1,000 litres of edible acorns for each mature tree and a single worker may be able to collect between 100-200 litres per day (Howes 1948:173). However, they are not a very predictable resource as for physiographic reasons they may not fruit at all for up to six years after a heavy crop (Dimbleby 1967:37). Oak does not have the same sort of potential as hazel for manipulation and control.

The Fen Basin

As the sea level rose as a result of the climatic amelioration which produced the retreat of the ice sheets, it obstructed the drainage of the fen basin, resulting in marsh formation on a major scale. Pollen diagrams and stratigraphic investigations (Clark et al. 1934; Clark and Godwin 1962; Godwin 1978:42-67; Worssam and Taylor 1969) indicate that the formation of lacustrine deposits in the Cambridge region must have been well under way by the Pre-Boreal and peat formation was already well developed in some areas by the Boreal.[3] Peatlands are unstable, dynamic ecological systems constantly changing and spreading, growing and eroding. By definition they are unbalanced systems in which the rate of production of organic material by living organisms exceeds the rate of decomposition and erosion. The result is the constant accumulation of an organic deposit, peat. As the peat blanket thickens with time, the surface vegetation becomes progressively more and more insulated from the underlying geology and consequently floristic change can be related, in a fairly straightforward way, to alterations in hydrology and the changing levels of the peat surface. Walker (1970) estimates the average rate of peat formation in British post-glacial hydroseres to have been somewhere in the region of 80-100 cm/century between 7,800 and 5,400 b.c.

Peatlands may be divided, broadly, into two basic types: (i) ombrotrophic peatlands, and (ii) minerotrophic peatlands (Moore and Bellamy, 1973:64-71; Mornsjö 1971). Each type is related to essential differences in hydrotopography, water movements and source and geomorphology. Ombrotrophic peatlands or bog peats receive their basic water supply directly from precipitation and are usually characterized by a pronounced deficiency of mineral nutrients. Minerotrophic peatlands receive their water supply from both precipitation and ground water or surface run-off and consequently have a high concentration of mineral nutrients. The overall primary productivity is largely dependent on the mineral content of the water supply which conditions the nature of the surface vegetation. Sphagnum plant communities are usually dominant in ombrotrophic peatlands while reedswamp is characteristic of minerotrophic peatlands and is capable of a far more rapid and vigorous growth. The East Anglian fens are a classic example of minerotrophic peatland. The eutrophic lake and marsh ecology which developed in the north of the Cambridge region was due to the vast amount of alklaine water and the nutrients contained in it, derived from the Cam-Ouse river catchment area. This area, in its natural state, would have an extremely high net primary productivity, possibly between 800-4,600 g/m^2/year, with the upper figure being more probable (Whittaker 1970:83). Such an area might be capable of providing 21-56 g/m^2/day of edible plant foods, a figure based on measurements for a temperate European grass swamp (Clarke 1976:464). Moore and Bellamy (1973:89-91) cite figures for a Scirpus lacustris dominated swamp in Germany as having an annual net production of 4,600 g/m^2 (46 metric tons/ acre) which far exceeds that of most agricultural crop production rates. The average wheat yield in a high production area (the Netherlands) is only 1,250 g/m^2/year (Moore and Bellamy 1973:91).

Plants exhibit distinct zonation with regard to water depth. Different species represent successive stages of the hydrosere as lakes gradually become shallower as a result of the accumulation of organic debris. The lower peat of the fen basin passed through three main stages during its ecological succession: (i) a predominantly open water lake/riverine stage, (ii) a growing over stage, and (iii) the formation of woody fen carr. At the growing over stage when the vegetation is dominated by reeds, biological production reaches a maximum (Westlake 1963). Some areas, particularly on the borders of the fenland, were extensively invaded by trees, the remains of which are frequently dug up out of the peats (Godwin and Clifford 1953; Godwin 1978:34). Walker (1970) emphasises that this ecological succession of fenlands is quite flexible and may frequently be reversed with changes in hydrology. In many cases the true climax of the hydrosere may not be terrestrial woodland but an ombrogenous bog.

There is no natural fen vegetation left in the Cambridge region today.
Areas such as Wicken fen (Plate 2) have been constantly disturbed in the
recent past and most other areas have been extensively drained. Wicken fen
and other contemporary fens can give us some idea of the nature and the productivity of the fenland in Boreal/Atlantic times. Rybnicek (1973) has argued
that one should expect a relatively uniform number of species, composition,
structure and habitat requirement in both present and past mire communities
due to their specific synecology. Out of the 261 vascular plants recorded
from Wicken fen, 141 are potentially edible (calculated from Walters 1967).
Wicken fen exhibits a patchwork of different vegetative communities dominated by Cladium, Molinia, herbs, sedges, grasses and bushes. Cladium
dominates areas of shallow water along with scattered individuals of Yellow
Loosestrife and Phragmites, maintaining itself by means of its vigorous and
extensive underground rhizomes. The Cladium fen is almost immediatly
followed by fen carr. The critical factor for the successful establishment
of these woody shrubs—alder, blackthorn, guelder rose, currant, birch and
hazel—is the height of the water table in winter (Tansley 1965:642). The surface of the fen is uneven as a result of differential peat growth and results
in a locally variegated habitat with species of different requirements in close
juxtaposition.

White (1932) in a study of the north-east Irish fens bordering on Lough
Neagh illustrates the complex degree of zonation that may exist in well developed fen communities with different zones dominated by one or more species forming local associations. Twenty separate associations were distinguished, related successively to the upper, middle and lower fen. This is
quite obviously a simplified picture as one would expect a high degree of
overlap and interchange between the different societies.

This horizontal zonation results in an extremely diversified plant community over comparatively short distances and, as Clarke (1976) emphasizes,
this is likely to represent an optimal potential resource. Club rush has a
potential yield of 46 metric tonnes/ha/year, its tubers, lower stems and seeds
being edible. This yield outstrips by 30% that of most cereals (Phillipson
1966:37).

The importance of these fen plant food resources is not only their extremely high potential productivity per unit area and rapid regeneration after harvesting, but also their availability in the winter, which in the deciduous forest
zone constitutes an ecological restriction. Deep water plants such as the
yellow and white water lily have storage organs which are available throughout the winter and provide seeds rich in endosperm. The totally edible water-
cress and the water chestnut would provide important sources of winter
greenery. In areas of shallower water water plantain, water parsnip, marsh
marigold and cress would be available and fringed by the productive sedge
communities providing rhizomes, edible greenery and stems throughout the
year and also the fruiting and nutting fen carr.

In the Cambridge region a major ecotone may be heuristically distinguished. An ecotone is a transitional zone between two or more diverse
communities and contains many of the organisms inhabiting both and in addition others characteristic of and restricted to the ecotone (Odum 1971:157).

The number of species and their population density may be greater than in surrounding areas. Such an area, therefore, would offer especially abundant plant and animal food resources. In the Cambridge region we may distinguish an ecotone running along the edge of the fen basin where it is adjacent to the 'dry' deciduous forest zone and the 'damp' deciduous forest of the boulder clay plateaux and river terrace areas (Plate 3 and Map C).

In view of the "cautionary tales' with regard to the archaeological use of the ecotone concept (Rhoades 1978), it is used in this study merely as a useful heuristic device in need of further investigation. Rhoades (1978:10) points out that the phenomenal status of the concept of an ecotone is the subject of a continuing debate amongst ecologists. The 'continuum school' denies that ecosystems must have boundaries. Whether or not the concept is applicable as an explanatory device would seem to depend on the level and type of ecosystem analysis being performed. In a rather broad regional context there can be little doubt that different communities do exist in relatively discrete areas and in some cases, such as between the fen and areas of surrounding higher land, these boundaries may be relatively well defined with some sort of transitional zone of interdigitating vegetable and animal communities which is largely governed in its spatial extent by differences in local topography. From the perspective of a least-cost economic strategy such an area might have been particularly favourable for human occupation and exploitation.

(v) Resource use schedule: Animal foods

Speaking in general terms, animal populations offer the best possibilities for exploitation if they have a high density, low mobility, high degree of aggregation and high meat and non-food yields. Lacking any reliable faunal evidence from excavated Mesolithic sites within the Cambridge region, we are forced to surmise as to the main sources of animal foods available to the local population on the basis of faunal data from sites outside the region; Star Carr (Clark 1954; 1972) and Thatcham (Wymer 1962). At these sites the main hunted species were aurochs, elk, red deer, roe deer, wild boar, beaver, birds and various small game species such as fox, badger and pine marten.

Among these, all the ungulate species tend to be predisposed towards a habitat type consisting of relatively open woodland in a state of succession with open clearings and an extensive ground cover rather than dense climax forests with a closed leaf canopy. According to Waterbolk (1968) the closed Atlantic deciduous forests positively discouraged ungulates because the impenetrably dense forest canopies would have shaded out the intermediate shrub and ground plant societies essential for browsing and grazing. This statement is probably too extreme as pollen diagrams from Hockham Mere and Peacock's Farm tend to suggest a persistent, if discontinuous, representation of herbaceous vegetation and high hazel values (Godwin and Tallantire 1951; Godwin 1934; 1960; Sims 1973). However, areas of dense deciduous forest probably did support significantly lower biomass densities than more open areas (cf. Mellars 1974:51-53). The fen area within the Cambridge region would have formed the only really extensive area of relatively open ground. The fen edge ecotone may have been an optimum resource zone for ungulates, especially in the late autumn and winter when most of the fen area may have been flooded and there would have been few other areas providing extensive quantities of green plant foods.

20

The preferred biotope for aurochs (Bos primigenius) seems to have been grasslands and lightly forested areas with marshy clearings (Heptner et al. 1966), and therefore we might expect to find them maximally abundant during the Pre-Boreal and Boreal periods and concentrated in the 'dry'deciduous forest with its less dense vegetative structure and in the fen edge ecotone regions during the Atlantic and relatively scarce elsewhere (Degerbøl 1964). The population may have risen and expanded with the onset of forest clearance during the Neolithic and the Bronze Age. The density and social behaviour or aurochs, an extinct species, remains problematic. On the basis of analogies with the morphologically similar North American bison we might expect relatively permanent social groups of four to six individuals with larger seasonal aggregations (c.40-200) (Roe 1970; Soper 1941). We might expect relatively limited movement in a temperate climatic regime, where seasonal disparities in the availability of foodstuffs would not be so marked. Price (1978:100) estimates the density of aurochs from the proportional representation of this species at Star Carr, assuming that it was hunted opportunistically along with red deer, as 0.56 animals/km^2. Historical documentation suggests that aurochs entered rut in early autumn and tended to have a much more restricted mobility in winter (Grzimek 1970). On ecological grounds we might expect aurochs to cluster in relatively warm and low lying areas such as the fen edge where green plant foods would be most abundant. Exploitation at this season may have been most desirable.

It is interesting to note the large number of finds of skeletons of aurochs, several with body wounds, documented from Scanian and Danish mires (Degerbøl and Fredskild 1970; Lilijegren and Welinder 1971). Such finds may be related to hunting activities, the animals being forced out into swampy areas to escape their human predators and subsequently drowning. A number of isolated skeletons have been recovered from peat deposits within the Cambridge region including a complete skeleton from Burwell fen and a skeleton from Littleport, dated by pollen analysis to the early Bronze Age (Higgs and Shawcross 1961).

The basis of a favourable habitat for elk (Alces alces) is provided by forest succession as in the Pre-Boreal and early Boreal (Peterson 1955:153). They decline in numbers as the forest reaches maturity and may have been rare or extinct by the early Atlantic[4].

Elk are large animals, adults weighing over 900 kg (Hosley 1949), and consequently require a large food intake. In summer a grown elk consumes 30-40 kg of green foods in a 24 hour period. In the first half of winter this may drop to 15-20 kg and may be as low as 8-12 kg in later winter (Egorov 1967). In spring the rich aquatic vegetation of lakes and streams provides their preferred diet (Peterson 1955). Heptner et al. (1966) record that Russian elk find c. 110 grass and herb species and c. 30 shrub species palatable, willow, birch, pine and juniper being preferred (Ahlén 1975). Pine twigs appear to form an especially important component of their diet during the winter. This may be related to their high protein, carotene and ascorbic acid content (Cowan et al. 1950).

Population densities are usually low, commonly between 1-3/1,000 ha., although they may be higher in game reserves (Bannikov 1970). Daily and seasonal movement is normally quite restricted, typically 0.5-1.0 km in winter and slightly more in summer (Battenberghe and Peek 1971). Seasonal movement is usually dependent on local ecological productivity and depth of winter snow cover. It may amount to no more than a few kilometres (Goddard 1970) or to much greater distances where topographical differences are more pronounced. In the Cambridge region we should expect seasonal movement, therefore, to be slight.

Elk are monogamous, although this does not involve pair bonding. The only constant social group is the mother and her young. The temporary male-female pair bonds are formed during the rutting season in September and October (Peterson 1955). Exploitation during the autumn and winter may have been most efficient as a result of the generally lower level of mobility. As elk require considerable quantities of surface water, the fen basin and the fen edge ecotone may have been their optimal habitat during the spring and summer, and they may have concentrated in the fen edge ecotone in winter.

Both aurochs and elk would have provided a large meat yield but their exploitation is likely to have been largely on a spasmodic and opportunistic basis because of their low population densities and limited degree of aggregation, especially in the case of the elk.

Red deer (Cervus elaphus) inhabit a wide variety of environments from open moorland to closed forests. Darling (1969:53) states that most of the food of the Scottish red deer consists of ground vegetation such as grasses, sedges and heather and available woodland is little used. A study of the rumen content of red deer in Jutland (Jensen 1968) demonstrates a greater use of browse foods, but the same basic dependence on grasses. Browse is an important food source in winter (McCullough 1969:47).

Population densities seem to range widely. Darling (1969) gives figures of 16 ha./animal, while for the Tokho valley, Yakutia, Egerov (1967) cites figures of 300 ha./animal. Darling suggests that it is impracticable to have a denser deer population than the present Scottish one and points out that higher densities in deer parks result in anti-social behaviour and poor physical conditions. The red deer that Darling studied maintained separate groupings of hinds and stags at all seasons of the year except during the early autumn rut. The size of the hind groups ranged between 5 and 200, while the stags maintained small flexible, unstructured groups with a loose and changing membership. Schloeth (1961) records that the only stable unit existing amongst the red deer in the Swiss National Park is the mother and her calf, sometimes with an occasional yearling. The same appears to be true in Yakutia (Egerov 1967). Most red deer live either in pairs or solitary. Edwards and Wallace (1927) record the same social groupings for Exmoor red deer. It is notable that all these examples refer to areas in which red deer live primarily in a lightly forested environment. The large Scottish herds recorded by Darling would seem to be either atypical or a product of essentially open ground conditions.

Seasonal movements of red deer are relatively well defined, being from upland areas in summer to lowland areas in winter, with dispersal over relatively extensive territories during the summer and congregation in smaller, sheltered areas during the winter (Lowe 1966). Studies of the North American

22

deer (Cervus canadensis) demonstrated that the summer territory may be up to ten times more extensive than that utilized during the winter (Mellars 1975: Table 3).

From these considerations we might expect to find red deer maximally important as a resource in autumn and winter, perhaps concentrating in the fen edge ecotone where a wide variety of herbs and browse would be available, and dispersing into other areas during the summer months.

Mitchell (1969) has documented a change from larger to smaller animals and correlated this with an associated change from the use of a primarily woodland habitat to that of a heathland habitat as a result of human influence. The performance of hill red deer as regards growth rates, fecundity, recruitment rates and density appears to be lower than in deer inhabiting lowland forest areas (cf. Clark 1972:27). We might expect, therefore, that the deer existing during the early Post-glacial period were a more productive resource than studies of contemporary deer populations would seem to suggest.

A figure of 4.0 red deer/km^2 is the approximate figure used by Clark (1972) to calculate deer biomass for the Star Carr population. However, animal population densities are notoriously hard to reconstruct. The modern data upon which prehistoric population estimates are based is complicated by the great spatial variation which exists and by having to account for differing environmental conditions. Clark's estimate is rather conservative in view of the deer biomass densities that Mellars (1975:50-53) cites for North American and Eastern European populations. A figure in the region of 6-9 deer/km^2 is perhaps more realistic giving a potential total population for the Cambridge region of between 15, 360 and 23, 040.

Using Clark's Star Carr data, 41 kg would seem an appropriate average weight for roe deer (for both sexes, as sexual dimorphism is not marked) and 190 kg for a red deer stag. The latter obviously offered far more potential in terms of meat weight alone as a food resource.

Roe deer are most abundant in mixed woodlands with a good deal of understorey vegetation, glades and clearings. They maintain much lower population densities in areas of closed forest (Tegner 1951; Prior 1968). In contrast to red deer they are browsers rather than grazers. The spreading Post-glacial deciduous forest may have favoured high roe deer densities. The gradual closing of this forest would have been unfavourable. We might expect that roe deer would have been most abundant in the Late-Boreal and early Atlantic, especially in the less dense 'dry' deciduous forest areas and in the fen edge ecotone. In general roe deer exhibit behavioural patterns similar to those of red deer as regards their mobility and dispersal in different seasons of the year, and they tend to be more concentrated in winter and more widely dispersed in summer (Prior 1968). Roe deer groups are generally smaller and more stable than those of red deer, ranging from a solitary individual to groups which range in size between two and ten individuals (Grzimek 1970). Economically, roe deer are likely to have been less important than red deer due to their smaller body size and generally lower degree of seasonal aggregation. However, their early sexual maturity and the high incidence of multiple births (Prior 1968) results in a high potential rate of increase and might allow a comparatively high annual cull without seri ously depleting populations.

Prior (1968) cites densities of between 11.0/km^2 and 21.2/km^2, while Darling (1964) suggests a figure of 10.0/km^2 for French deer forests. The potential range is obviously quite wide. Using these figures we can estimate a potential total roe deer population for the Cambridge region as between 25,600 and 54,272 animals.

On the basis of historical documentation the ideal habitat for wild boar appears to be deciduous forests and moist marshy areas (Oloff 1951; Fleming, 1972). Coniferous forests, open grasslands and dry soil habitats prove unfavourable. Their major food consist of nuts, especially acorns, roots, herbs and grasses. Howes (1948:173) cites historical accounts from central Portugal where acorns were a primary autumnal food source on which the boar were fattened, 5.3 litres of acorns being said to produce one pound of pork. If predators are eradicated boar populations seem to increase dramatically. Fleming (1972) quotes very high figures for eleventh century boar populations in Essex: 40-190/km^2. The Atlantic deciduous forest may have offered a very favourable habitat for boar. The drier and more pine-dominated Pre-Boreal and Boreal forest would have been less suitable.

There appear to be marked oscillations in general population numbers from year to year as a result of disease, variable food supply and predation. Population densities are again quite variable, ranging from 20-250/ha. (Oloff 1951; Bay-Petersen 1978:123).

The fen area comprises approximately 35% of the Cambridge region. Certain animals would have been abundant only here such as beaver and otter. Beavers live in lodges where they are able to dam streams or along river banks and lakesides. In spring and summer the food intake consists mainly of water plants and the leaves and twigs of water-loving plants such as aspen, birch and willow. In winter large quantities of bark from all deciduous trees, except alder, are consumed (Wilsson 1971). Beavers tend to be more dispersed in summer, with lower body and fat weights, but aggregate during the winter in their lodges. The number of animals varies but ranges between 5 and 12/lodge. Beavers lose little fat in winter and 30-40% of the live body weight at this time of the year consists of deposited fat. This falls to about 10% in summer when the animals are freely moving about and expending energy at a greater rate (Novakowski 1967; Aleksiuk and Cowan 1969). Innis (1956) cites population densities of 40+/1,000 ha. for Canada in good years, while Novakowoski (1967) estimates beaver density as 90/1,000 ha. for populations in the Mackenzie delta. The complex and intricate system of lakes, rivers and streams which existed in the fen area in Atlantic times may have provided an ideal beaver habitat and exploitation would have been optimal during the autumn and winter when their mobility is low, aggregation high and fat yields greatest.

There can be no doubt that fish productivity was extremely high in the fen area, especially during the Late-Boreal and Atlantic periods. Historical sources document the importance of fishing in the life of the medieval fenland monasteries and villages. At Doddington there are records of a fishery returning 27,150 eels per annum, while 17,000 eels per annum are recorded at Littleport (Darby 1940). A manor of Ramsey abbey in the north-west of the Cambridge region made a profit solely on account of its return of eels. In

A.D. 974 twenty fishermen gave 60,000 eels each for the use of the brethren. A chronicler wrote of Ramsey mere: "though but fishers and fowlers cease neither by day nor by night to frequent it, yet is there always no little store of fish", pike of "extraordinary great size" being a frequent catch along with perch, bream, roach and tench (Darby 1940). Such resources would have been of primary importance during the summer months due to the inaccessibility of much of the fenland in winter owing to widespread flooding and the tendency of fish to remain on the lake bed whilst it is cold. Wildfowl, too, was extremely plentiful in the fen areas, the variety being as remarkable as the quantity. In the twelfth century Thomas of Ely wrote: "There are numberless geese, fiscedulae, coots, dabchicks, watercrows, herons and ducks of which the number is indeed great. At mid winter, or when the birds moult their quills, I have seen them caught by the hundred, and even by the three hundred more or less " (Darby 1940:36). This is evidently an all-year-round resource, although we might expect exploitation to have taken place mainly in spring and summer.

Small game, such as fox, badger, pine marten, wolf, hare and lynx can be expected to be distributed more or less uniformly over the entire area with relatively limited mobility.

From a consideration of the above discussion we can tentatively produce a table (Table 1) showing the expected dietary importance of resources in the Pre-boreal, Boreal and the Atlantic periods, the seasons when these resources would be most abundant and therefore most easily exploited, and the areas where we might expect to find the greatest spatial concentration of these food resources. From this table we can postulate economic seasons relating to the exploitation of specific resources and the areas in which we might expect to find settlement at a particular time during the year. We should hope to define a best-fit pattern of economic exploitation which minimizes conflicts between the availability of different resources in different areas at approximately the same time. We may discern four basic economic seasons. In autumn the exploitation of hazelnut/bracken root/acorn and fungi associations may have been or primary importance. Such foods were easily gathered and has a high potentiality for storage. These plant food resources might be supplemented by aurochs and elk which may have been especially important in the Boreal. Red and roe deer beginning to aggregate for the rut would become increasingly important as the season progressed and plant foods became depleted. Winter would have been the critical period for the survival of a population practising a hunting and gathering economy. The deciduous forest had, ecologically speaking, closed down. Green plant foods, where they could be found, would be of critical nutritional importance. Stored nuts and fruits such as dried apples and rosehips may have been used. Animal derived foods would become of great importance especially during the Boreal when there would have been fewer easily storable plant foods available. Red deer and boar may have been the primary staples supplemented by aurochs and elk in the Boreal and roe deer in the Atlantic. Beaver, aggregating in their winter lodges would have provided valuable sources of animal fats. Plant foods would increase in importance during the spring along with fish, birds and small game. Big game may still have been of primary importance. In summer and early autumn plant foods, fish and waterfowl may have been the most attractive and easily exploited resources. Large game animals may have only made a small contribution to the diet. Fig. 9 is a tentative representation of such a seasonal exploitation pattern.

(vi) Mesolithic man and environmental manipulation

The traditional concept of the Mesolithic is that of a period in which small, ill-equipped populations struggled constantly in order to survive and did not need, or were not able, to alter their natural environment (Godwin 1956:332). Since the early 1960's several authors have begun seriously to question this assumption (Rankine and Dimbleby 1960; Dimbleby 1962; Simmons 1969; Smith 1970). Simmons (1969) and Smith (1970) have discussed evidence which suggests that quite extensive land areas may have been cleared during the later Mesolithic (pollen zones VI-VIIa). If fire was used either deliberately or accidentally, the areas cleared would be out of all proportion to the size of the population responsible. On poor, acidic and easily podzolised soils such as those of the Breckland district in the north-east of the Cambridge region, repeated burning, coupled with the effects of animal grazing, might prevent forest regeneration which would be naturally slow on such soils and ultimately lead to the heath formation that exists in the area today.

At Oakhanger (Hampshire), Dimbleby (1960) suggests that the evidence from the pollen diagrams relates to an increasing destruction of the forest cover during the successive occupations of the site. He suggests that increasing soil acidity might have resulted in a loss of structure and soil stability. It is evident that the effect of man upon the natural vegetation depends not only on the intensity and duration of his practices but also upon soil fertility. Even relatively brief periods of deforestation could lead to a rapid decline in soil fertility where soils are naturally poor. The soils of Breckland are noted for their impoverishment and high permeable nature. This situation is exacerbated by this region being one of the driest in Southern Britain (Plate 4). (Farrow 1915; R. Clarke 1960; Macdonald and Watt 1938). Coarse sandy soils are especially prone to leaching and therefore are susceptible to a relatively rapid loss of mineral nutrients from the upper levels of the soil profile. Dimbleby (1962:15-16, 21) points out that it is quite possible that soil deterioration leading to podzolization may occur even under a covering of mature deciduous forest so that the influence of the parent material on the soil profile may be of primary importance so that a decline in fertility is not necessarily a result of human influence, although deforestation would have hastened this process. Godwin (1944) correlated the arrival of ericoid species in the Breckland region with Neolithic forest clearance and soil podzolisation. This might well have been the culmination of a long series of human interferences with the natural vegetation dating from early Atlantic times. Perrin, Willis and Hodge (1964) have demonstrated by radiocarbon measurements on humus that podzolization was well under way by 910 ± 100 b.c.

Mellars (1975, 1976b) and Mellars and Reinhart (1978:260-263) have put considerable emphasis on the effect of forest fires on subsistence and settlement patterns. Mellars and Reinhardt stress six chief benefits: (i) increasing the mobility of human groups and thereby reducing time and energy expenditure, (ii) improving hunting conditions by reducing the amount of escape cover and perhaps allowing communal hunting strategies, (iii) increasing animal biomass, (iv) increasing the relative growth rate of young animals and the size of adults, (v) increasing the ability of human populations to render animal movements predictable, and (vi) by increasing the yield of plant food resources (Mellars and Reinhardt 1978:260). In general the overall productivity of the area would be increased and the efficiency with which food resources could be extracted. Mellars (1976b) suggests that a maximum concentration of animals may be achieved by creating a patchwork of burnt areas which would create a number of distinct ecotones between areas of burnt open ground and those with an undisturbed vegetation cover. The Breckland area in the north east of the Cambridge region with its relatively poor soil structure preventing rapid forest regeneration and less dense understorey vegetation may have been particularly suited to successful fire-setting.

The tranchet axe must have had a considerable potential for tree-felling and wood working. Some are of considerable weight. The majority of these axes fall into relatively close size limits dictated by the diameter of the enclosing wood or antler haft. Jacobi (1976) has shown that most of these axes cluster between 110 and 130 mm in length and represent only the stubs of axes discarded when whittling down had brought the blade as close as was tolerable to its mounting. Virtually all the axes from the Cambridge region are isolated surface finds. Significantly, no hoards are known.[5] This might indicate small scale use on an individual basis. Map E shows the distribution of tranchet axes within the Cambridge region. It will be immediately obvious that the main concentration occurs in the north-east of the region with two sub-clusters: (1) a comparatively nucleated cluster in the southern fens around Burwell, Swaffham and Quy, and (2) a more diffuse cluster centered upon Breckland in the vicinity of Icklingham and Mildenhall.

Proceeding from the null hypothesis of randomness the chi-square test was performed to see if the distribution of tranchet axes could be shown to cluster over a number of soil types and ecological zones recognized within the Cambridge region. The major soil types and ecological zones were defined on page 6 (see Tables 3 and 4).

There were far more axes found on fen soils than would be expected if they were distributed at random, and hardly any upon the boulder clay or rendzina/loam soils. The chi-square statistic was well above the 0.001% significance level. Further comparison was undertaken between the fen and Breckland. χ^2 had a value of 1.5424, which at 1° of freedom was not significant. The intensity of activities involving tranchet axes in the fens and in the Breckland region was equivalent although it would be unwise to conclude that the nature of the activities was necessarily similar.

If we assume that tranchet axes were used in forest clearance and wood-working and that the lightly forested Breckland zone would be particularly amenable to such activities, we would expect a clustering of axes within the region, and this is certainly the case. Comparison of the number of axes discovered upon Breckland soils and those found upon loam soils revealed that the expected frequency/unit area was virtually reversed, with 39 axes occurring upon Breckland soils where we should only expect 10.89 if distributed at random, and 9 occurring on loam soils where we should expect 53.80.

Similarly, chi-square tests affirmed that tranchet axes were not distributed at random but clustered within the "dry" deciduous forest zone and the fen edge ecotone. Further comparison between these two zones by means of the chi-square test showed that there were more axes in the fen edge ecotone and less in the dry deciduous forest zone than we should expect. x^2 was significant at the 0.01% level. Furthermore x^2 was positively significant, well above the 0.001% level, in a comparison between axe distribution in the fen vegetation and "wet" deciduous forest zones, with far more occurring in the former than we should expect from the null hypothesis that the axes are distributed at random.

The fen-edge ecotone embraces areas of the highly acid and permeable Breckland soils and waterlogged fen areas. It is precisely in this area that, in the section upon settlement location, we have postulated that relatively large winter occupation settlements might have been established which would obviously require large quantities of timber for fuel and for the construction of shelters requiring the use of heavy core axes. Settlement might shift in summer, with the centre of the fen basin being the main favoured area. Fuel would not be so significant and hence the less dense concentration of axes. Those axes found within the dry deciduous forest zone may relate to autumnal settlement and associated land clearance, the main reasons for which will be discussed below.

It is interesting to compare this analysis of tranchet axe distribution with that of Mellars and Reinhardt (1978) for southern England. Their study related the spatial distribution of three artifact types, microliths, tranchet axes and pebble maceheads, to major geological formations. All three artifact types were quantitatively more significant on coarsely textured sandy soils supporting 'dry' deciduous forest. However, both the tranchet axe and the pebbled macehead distribution was "less selective" with respect to the underlying geology and associated soil types than the microlith distribution which was heavily concentrated on the coarse sandy soils of the Lower Greensand (Mellars and Reinhardt 1978:276, fig. 6). Mellars and Reinhardt attempt to explain this distribution by suggesting that the microliths were primarily utilized in relation to hunting activities which, on ecological grounds similar to those suggested here for the Breckland region, may have been particularly productive in areas supporting 'dry' deciduous forest, especially if coupled with deliberate burning and opening out of such areas. They further suggest that as tranchet axes may be related to a far wider range of activities this might explain its wider distribution. In the Cambridge region the tranchet axe distribution shows a similar preference for coarse sandy soils supporting areas of 'dry' deciduous forest and also for the adjacent fen edge ecotone, but contrasts in that they are only sparsely represented in others areas with heavier silt, loam and clay soils. This may be indicative of a more selective use in this case (see Table 4). By contrast the distribution of Neolithic axes is far more dispersed (Map G and Table 4). The distribution of pebble maceheads, albeit few in number is very similar to that of the tranchet axes (Map E and Table 4). The precise function of these artifacts is in doubt. One possibility is that they represent weights for digging sticks, on the basis of ethnographic analogy (Oswalt 1976:56-8). However as Rankine (1953:188) points out, the perforation is too small in some cases. Another possible use is as arrow shaft straighteners or as some sort of hafted percussion tools (Rankine 1953:186). If they did function as weights for digging sticks this might explain their distribution in fenland skirt areas where a wide variety of rhizomes and other vegetable foods would be available for exploitation. The distribution of isolated surface finds of microliths (Map G) and Mesolithic sites with microliths (Map F and Chapter V) indicates a similar pattern, which suggested an extensive use of the Breckland region and the bordering fen areas. The whole pattern appears to be far more selective than that suggested by Mellars and Reinhardt (1978) for southern England, although this may be solely the product of a much smaller scale of analysis.

The relationship of the four main hunted animal species, red and roe deer, pig and Bos (in approximately equal numbers at Thatcham)[6] and man implies a stable and successful adaptation lasting for almost 5,000 years with a stable predator/prey balance. In order to exploit animal populations optimally it is necessary (1) to operate a culling policy which is not likely to deplete the herds, (2) to increase the browsing potential, (3) to control the position of the herds, and (4) to reduce the numbers of predators. Herd productivity may be increased by the selective culling of male animals in polygamous species such as red deer. Young animals, too, may be selectively killed as many of these are not essential to the maintenance of the herd and represent a low investment in terms of vegetation consumed/unit quantity of meat. It seems in no way improbable that red deer herds within the Cambridge region may have been husbanded in a way not dissimilar to that in which they are treated in deer parks today. It would, however, be a mistake to think in terms of red deer based economies such as Jarman (1972a) has suggested. It is feasible to think in terms of specific seasonal site positions so as to integrate both plant food gathering and the exploitation of a number of red deer herds at different times.

As Mellars points out (1975, 1976b), increased browse for ungulates, and hence a higher biomass, may be effectively produced by burning off the forest canopy and stimulating glade development and larger open areas. Mellars documents this practice amongst North American aboriginal populations. Experiments have shown that the weight of browse available three years after burning an area of forest is increased five-fold (Dills 1970). By means of continual burning of regions within established deer territories the movement of the animals might have been rendered more predictable. Such a situation is probable in the Pennines (Jacobi 1978b), and the main microlith concentrations can frequently be correlated with hills commanding extensive views wh ch may have been used for observing herd movements (Jacobi 1978b:325).

Hazel exhibits very high values in early Post-glacial pollen diagrams from the Cambridge region and most other areas of Britain. This has been regarded as a climatic effect but Smith (1970) suggests that human activities may have hastened this autogenic process. Smith describes hazel as a "fire climax" vegetation owing to its capacity to survive burning and quickly colonize burned areas, flowering and producing edible nuts after three to four years. Hazel scrub might therefore be maintained and encouraged in this way without specific propagation. Increasing deer biomass might be an accidental result of this form of control over vegetation patterns and might be conceived as a

29

positive feedback mechanism stimulating increasingly frequent burning over larger and larger areas. Jacobi et al. (1976) suggest that, particularly in the later stages of the Mesolithic, closed tree cover above 360 m on the Pennines was suppressed by frequent burning, encouraging the spread of hazel and higher deer biomass densities. Whether such a situation took place in the Breckland region remains largely problematic, although Sim's studies (1973, 1978) at Hockham Mere demonstrate that this is a very real possibility.

In commercial production hazel reaches a fruiting peak between 15 and 50 years after planting, but for high yields the plants require frequent coppicing (Howes 1948:183; Masefield et al. 1971:26). Rich, heavy soils are not suitable as these tend to induce too much wood growth at the expence of nut production. Light, dry soils such as those of the Breckland region and the Greensand of the Weald are best. Hazel nuts may have been a particularly important food source as they offer considerable potential for storage and have relatively high contents of protein (9-12%) and fat (36-64%) (Howes 1948: 23). In this respect they form a useful complementary resource to acorns, which have a protein content of 7-4%, a low fat content (4.6%) and a high carbohydrate content (67.8%) (ibid., 23). Acorns seem to have been widely used as a food source in Europe during historic times as a flour substitute (Clark 1952:59). The North American indians utilized them on a large scale and in California they were a staple (Driver 1964:91).

Jacobi (1978a) makes the point that even allowing for only 10% of hazel flowers going on to fruit and only 10% of the fruit escaping predation by rodents, and assuming that only 30% of the remainder may have been harvested, their potential for supporting human populations far outstrips any estimate based on ungulate populations. He goes on to suggest that hazel nuts might provide, at a conservative estimate, 25% of the total diet for a minimum group of four families for four of the winter months and that sufficient could be harvested within $\frac{1}{4}$-1 mile of an occupation site in the Wealden area of southern England during the whole of pollen zone VI (Jacobi 1978a:82-3). Thomas (1972) has similarly hypothesized the importance of the pinion nut harvest to Shoshonean subsistence and settlement patterns in the Great Basin of the American South-West.

The removal of the natural forest canopy might also have the additional effect of stimulating the spread of bracken, the roots of which might form another important food resource during the autumn and winter. It is easily stored and like hazel nuts has high nutritional value, being rich in carbohydrates and protein (Hedrick 1972:470).

Simmons and Dimbleby (1974) have argued that ivy may have played an important role in the later Mesolithic economy of north-west Europe. Ivy is conceived as a possible fodder crop used to attract deer to areas of human occupation during the winter when green vegetation would be scarce.

Sims (1973) has discussed the pollen sequence from Hockham Mere and suggests it may represent Mesolithic land clearance. There appears to be decreased forest cover during pollen zone VIc (438-430 cms) with an increase in the pollen of Corylus and a decline in the pollen of elm, oak and birch. Significantly, there is a peak in the pollen of Hedera (ivy) between 440 and 437 cms, above which there is a sharp fall. Two peaks occur in the pollen of plants usually associated with open treeless areas - Plantago lanceolata, Plantago major/media, Compositae, Rumex acetosella, Chenopodicae - and in bracken spores. These peaks are separated by a temporary increase in Gramineae pollen.

Such a sequence by no means provides unequivocal evidence of an anthropogenic origin. The human associations of species such as Plantago lanceolata have probably been overstressed in the past. Such as species is likely to colonize open ground, whatever its origin. It is possible that such an effect might be produced in areas disturbed solely by animals frequently using the same grazing areas, watering places and traditional paths of movement. The pollen diagrams from Shippea Hill (Clark and Godwin 1962) for the Mesolithic occupation exhibit a decline in hazel pollen and an increase in the pollen of herbaceous plants coupled with a slight decline in tree pollen. We might expect such an effect in the disturbed environment which would inevitably be found around an occupation site, with some land clearance coupled with an increase in open air species.

In contrast, at Hockham Mere there is no positive evidence of settlement within the specific area from which the pollen samples were obtained, and therefore, the processes resulting in the distinctive pollen diagrams would seem to be different from those operating at Shippea Hill. It is indeed tempting to view the diagrams as evidence of land clearance, possibly by fire, stimulating hazel and bracken growth and that of other plants suitable for red deer browsing, possibly combined with the selective collection of ivy, in a sophisticated pattern of herd control.

In conclusion, it is suggested here that Mesolithic subsistence within the Cambridge region included broad knowledge of the efficient storage, harvesting, and reproductive control of plants such as hazel and bracken. Control of the forest ecology may have been effected by the use of fire coupled with forest husbandry - pruning and clearance by means of the tranchet axe. Control over game herds is perfectly feasible by stimulating browse in restriced areas. Both systems were complementary and could be integrated at certain seasons (autumn and winter) within the subsistence and settlement regime. The Breckland region would be the ideal area for such a pattern to developbecause it was here that vegetation could be most easily manipulated and that our postulated primary autumnal seasonal staples, hazel and bracken, would have been commonest initially. It is clear that man/plant/animal relationships were intricate and would fluctuate with time in complex and changing subsistence relationships. Land clearance designed in the long term to promote hazel growth might have had the short term effect of increasing deer biomass, which might have led to a temporary increase in hunting. Conversely burning, designed primarily to control herd movement, might had led to an increase in hazel.

(vii) Settlement Location: Theoretical Considerations and Predictive Models

In this section regularities resulting in settlement locations at specific points will be discussed and a set of hypotheses and predictions will be erected.

31

The location of settlements amongst hunter-gatherers may be viewed as the outcome of a set of decisions related to a number of goals which need to be fulfilled (Jochim 1976:50). The primary determinent behind settlement location is undoubtedly the subsistence requirements of the social unit, involving seasonal moves relating to fluctuating resources and intraseasonal moves due to the over-exploitation of the area immediately surrounding the site. Any settlement location attempts to resolve conflicts between the differential availability and spatial proximity of food and other resources such as water, fuel and building materials. Effort conservation and distance minimization are factors of overriding importance. Protection from the elements, and a concern for the texture and dryness of the ground surface and for a view of game movements may be of primary significance within the bounds of a feasible area delimited by subsistence considerations. Sites might be chosen near to a water supply, but not so near as to frighten the game away.

The greater the security of a resource, the greater its "pull" on settlement location. Jarman (1972b) notes that site location is likely to be nearest to the most static and most reliable resource, which in our case we have suggested may have been plant foods. The higher the prestige of a resource the lower its "pull" on settlement location because it will not be of primary significance in calorific terms. A sedentary situation might be desirable from the point of view of minimum effort for site re-location, but it conflicts with regional resource pulls and minimum energy expenditure in subsistence activities. Temporary satellite extraction camps are one possible answer to resolve this situation.

Vita Finzi and Higgs (1970) have demonstrated the regularity with which sites are placed on the margins of two differing ecological resource zones (ecotone situations) thus enabling the exploitation of a wide and diversified range of natural resources.

Clarke (1968, 1972) and Williams, Thomas and Bettinger (1973) have emphasized the need to search for regularities in site location in terms of polythetic sets as the use of a monothetic criterion will only adequately reflect one or several of the many goals which any settlement pattern hopes to fulfill.

Utilizing our hypothetical table of predicted seasonal resource schedules and areas in which certain resources are most abundant (Table 1), we may set up a series of specific predictions to which, if our assumptions are correct, the settlement pattern should conform.

General considerations

1. The majority of large, relatively permanent, sites should be in the fen edge ecotone. These may represent primarily winter occupation.

2. The "pull" of the vast range of resources to be exploited in the fen basin would be very great throughout the year, and especially during the summer months.

3. We should expect sites to be grouped like petals around the fen basin, with elongated territories embracing adjacent forest areas. Contact between these social territories might help to even out any disparity in local resource distribution. This locational regularity has been noted'

32

for Iron Age, Roman and Romano-British settlement patterns (Phillips 1970; Hall 1977).

4. Permanent settlement might theoretically be possible with a comparatively low population density, but this is unlikely in view of the varying resource potential of different areas of the region at different seasons, given an assumption of effort minimization and a desire for a variety of subsistence resources.

5. Annual territories are likely to be linear or elliptical, criss-crossing the fen basin and forest areas, rather than circular.

6. The Breckland zone, as a result of its fruitful potential for human inter-ference to increase the available food supply and its less dense under-storey vegetation cover, is likely to have been extensively utilized for both hunting and gathering.

Two alternative models for settlement location may be erected: (i) a permanent base camp in the fen edge ecotone with satellite seasonal extraction camps at a maximum distance of 10 km to which all, or only a part, of the population might move due to the need to minimize effort; or (ii) we might expect winter settlement locales to be situated on the margins of the fen in order to exploit the most stable and static resource, green plant foods, which would be of critical nutritional importance. The wide availability of surface water would mean that this would not be a critical factor in site location. Surface elevation would be an important factor in the choice of any specific location due to the possibility of flooding. Small rises within the immediate area of fenland or on higher surrounding ground might be chosen (Plate 5). Red deer, roe deer, boar, beaver and other game animals would be likely to concentrate in such a region, seeking shelter during the winter, and could be easily and efficiently exploited. The Breckland fen edge area might be especially suitable for winter settlement due to the proximity to possible stored sources of food resulting from autumnal gathering activities, the sandy soils also providing a warm base for occupation.

In spring the same, or a similar, situation might be occupied with in-creasing emphasis on the plant foods, fish and wildfowl to be found in such an ecotone situation. Alternatively sites might be made within the "wet" deciduous forest zone in order to exploit fresh buds, shoots and flowers and big game such as red and roe deer and aurochs which might be moving into such an area.

We would expect to find summer settlement in the heart of the fenland for the optimal exploitation of plant, fish and fowl resources. Many sites might be adjacent to meres and rivers. Ridges of high ground, preferably sandy, might be the preferred settlement locales in order to afford protection against summer flooding. Sites might include the 'fen islands' or areas of higher ground surrounding the fen basin within the two-hour territory, in order to broaden further the subsistence potential.

Alternatively, summer camps might be situated within the heart of the "wet" deciduous forest region in order to exploit the wide range of plant and animal resources available. No doubt central areas of the fen basin would represent optimal summer locales within the Cambridge region. However, unless the total population was small it would not be possible for all human

33

groups to exploit this area simultaneously and it is likely that in the summer the fen basin and "wet" deciduous forest ecological zones were both utilized by the same or different social groups.

Autumn settlement might well be confined to the "dry" deciduous forest zone in order to exploit acorn/bracken/hazel plant associations, and the roe deer and boar which would be primarily concentrated here. Sites with a view of game movements and areas with dry sandy subsoil might be chosen. Sites should be near to rivers and other sources of water but not positioned immediately adjacent to them due to the possibility of frightening the game; they would instead be within half a mile or five minutes walk.

Model 2, Fig. 11, shows some of the hypothetical expected seasonal movements in an 'optimal' pattern of seasonal exploitation. Of course there is an infinite variety of specific locational choices and the dichotomy between the static situation (model 1) and the mobile position (model 2) is entirely artificial. In practice one would expect a large number of intermediate, partially mobile and partially static, extractive economic patterns to develop. The purpose here is to suggest very broadly the range of possible alternatives.

(viii) Population

Factors of natural environment do not automatically determine population density and distribution. The spatial and temporal configurations of population represent adjustment to these factors by means of decisions. The goals guiding these decisions are of primary importance. The provision of food with the minimum of effort and cost to the human group of one of the most important of these goals. A primary problem is the relationship of food availability (carrying capacity) to population density. It is not sensible to think in terms of Malthusian or maximum potential population estimates owing to the annual elasticity of resource fluctuation leading either to over-exploitation of food resources or the death of certain individuals (Hayden 1972). Birdsell (1957) has suggested that 'primitive' human populations have the potential to double with every generation, in the case of the Australian aborigines every sixteen years, unless there are artificial limitations such as infanticide and lactation taboos. We might expect the population to exist in equilibrium while exploiting only 30-40% of the total food resources available (Hasson 1975). Resource oscillations and cycles operate at three levels to control the population of any area: (i) the annual cycle with seasons in which few resources are available; (ii) successive annual oscillations with bad or lean years occurring periodically; (iii) disastrous years or runs of years in which factors (i) and (ii) are exacerbated by climatic or other factors at crucial times.

From modern ethnographic studies it is clear that tolerance levels exist in hunting and gathering societies beyond which population cannot grow. There is a clear contrast between actual carrying capacity and that culturally defined (Wobst 1974).

The greater the degree of spatial concentration of resources, the greater the yield of a specific site and the larger the possible coresident group. Changes in group size, therefore, can be related to the changing spatial contiguity of resources. Eskimo groups aggregate for winter sealing (Damas 1968), while the Hadza accumulate round water holes in the dry season where berries occur in large numbers (Woodburn 1968). The larger the spatial dispersion of population that exists the more the possibilities of food procurement and the greater the differentiation of labour possible. In addition there is less danger of losing resources to competing predators or to other human groups. Populations must aggregate for reasons of reproductive viability. Wobst (1974), by means of computer simulations and ethnographic evidence, has postulated a minimum size for hunter-gatherer mating networks of 175-475 people, the latter figure being the more probably. Hunter-gatherer populations often aggregate at specific times when resources are abundant for social purposes such as gift exchange, mating, reaffirmation of kinship ties and exchange of ideas. In the Cambridge region we might expect large social gatherings to take place in summer and/or autumn. The highly productive resource potential of the fen basin in summer, with readily available food sources, might afford very good opportunities for social gatherings. Archaeologically we should expect to find large sites covering an extensive area. In autumn large sites might exist in the Breckland region. Social motivation for seasonal aggregation would coincide with the need for large numbers of people to group together and store large quantities of hazel nuts, acorns and bracken roots for the winter months. These autumnal aggregates might divide into two or three smaller units occupying the most sheltered and productive areas in winter - the fen edge ecotone. In spring one might expect an increase in mobility due to renewed resource potential in the deciduous forest zones and these might be reflected in further social division.

Clark's (1972) estimates for the Pre-Boreal population density of Britain range from $15/600$ km^2 to $20/300$ km^2 or $0.03-0.07$/km^2. The area of the region studied is 2560 km^2, giving an upper limit to the total population in the range of 64-162 people. This is not within Wobst's parameters for reproductive viability. However during the Atlantic climatic maximum food resources, especially plant foods would be more abundant than in the Boreal and we can expect a higher total population in the range of 90-230 people. The extremely productive nature of the fen basin might arguably support a greater density of population than any other region of similar size in southern Britain during the late Atlantic.

We would expect population to increase linearly with time owing to the wider availability of subsistence products. This should be reflected in the archaeological record by a greater number of sites attributable to the Atlantic as opposed to the Boreal period.[7]

CHAPTER V

A CONSIDERATION OF THE MESOLITHIC MATERIAL

Earlier sites 8,500–6,800 b.c. (Map F)

There are six sites that can attribute with some probability to this phase, entirely on typological grounds based on a sequential division of microlith forms into earlier broad blade forms and later narrow blade forms. Virtually all the material comes from old surface collections which are frequently mixed with Neolithic and Bronze Age material. The collections suffer from a severe sampling bias towards recognisable or atypical tool classes. Debitage, flakes, unretouched blades and cores are generally under-represented. Little of this material has been published or has undergone any systematic analysis.

Home Heath, Lackford, T.L. 782.712 (Todd 1947)

This is the only excavated early site from the region and is the only one in which we can attribute any reliability to the sample of artifacts retained. The excavation was conducted privately by Todd in 1947 and much of the material is in the British Museum.

The site is situated on a narrow sandy gravel ridge and is near to the confluence of the river Lark and a major tributary. Here a small area of fen might afford plant, fowl and fish resources and a watering place for animals. Fig. 12 represents the site territory. Approximately 20% of the one-hour territory and 30% of the two-hour territory consisted of pine/birch/hazel mixed forest. The rest of the territory might have consisted of more open, lighter, park woodland dominated by pine, hazel and bracken. The site was well positioned to integrate a variety of resources.

Fig. 13 shows a diagrammatic section of the structure investigated by Todd and Fig. 14 is a plan of the excavation. Todd dug an area of approx. 80 sq. ft. and revealed the remains of a tent structure covering an area of 49 sq. ft. with a curved base. One main hearth, 2 x $1\frac{1}{4}$ ft., was situated towards the front of the structure and there were two smaller burned areas near to the walls of the structure. If we apply the usual formulae for estimating prehistoric populations (Naroll 1962, Cook and Heizer 1968, Weisnner 1974) existing within structures, it is clear that the Lackford 'tent' would not be large enough to support even a minimal social unit of two adults and two children. It is best, therefore, to interpret the structure as a windbreak perhaps delimiting and sheltering a working and cooking area. The area excavated by Todd was comparatively small and it is obvious that significant quantities of flint debris covered a much more extensive area of Home Heath.

Approximately 5,000 artifacts were recovered from the excavation, the majority of this material being debitage. Below is an analysis of the flint industry (after Jacobi 1976).

```
cores - 68
core flakes - 104
scrapers - 54 convex, 1 hollow
truncated flakes - 10
burins - 2
tranchet axes - 1
axe sharpening flakes - 1
utilised flakes - 20
micro burins - 9
hammerstones - 2
flakes - 110
blades retouched along one or two sides - 18
fabricators - 2
saws - 5
microliths - 57
    1a - 26
    1ac - 17
    1b - 6
    1bc - 1
    2a - 1
    2b - 1
    3a - 1
    4 - 4
unclassified - 1   (see Fig.32)
```

The most numerous microliths were the obliquely blunted points. An isolated lump of resin came from the site indicating the collection of elm or birch bark for resin used for mounting arrow points and barbs. The extensive nature of the industry implies a relatively long occupation. The presence of micro burins may indicate the manufacture of microliths on the site. It is important to note that here, as at most Mesolithic sites, the microlithic component forms a relatively small proportion of the industry. The large number of scrapers indicates the importance of hide and/or plant processing activities. Mellars (1976a) broadly divides mesolithic sites into a three-fold typology: Type A—microlith dominated assemblages. These are usually very small sites. Type B–'Balanced assemblages' with a microlithic component of between 30% and 60% amongst retouched tool classes and a relatively high proportion of flake and blade scrapers (25-50%). Type C–Scraper dominated assemblages, though there are few sites that actually fall into this category. Mellars makes the point that the vast majority of the earlier Mesolithic sites fall into his class B, while later Mesolithic sites tend to be more specialised. The Lackford site would seem to fit into this scheme very neatly with its rather generalized industry indicative of a wide range of different activities.

Some of the obliquely blunted points (classes 1a and 1ac) may have formed components of sickles and/or harvesting knives, meeting the pressing need for efficient reaping of the seeds, leaves and stems of various plant food resources. The serrated blades from the site, interestingly enough, have silica gloss and could have served a similar purpose. The hammerstones may have been used for cracking nuts or for grinding the tubers and roots of plants in order to makes them palatable by destroying the fibrous structure.

Evidence from the site territory and our hypothesized distribution of seasonal resources might suggest an autumn or a spring occupation. In the absence of any faunal evidence it is not possible to test this proposition further.

Cavenham Heath T.L. 760.720 (general area)

A large collection of surface finds exists in Cambridge Museum, comprising 17 microblades, cores, large numbers of blades or blade fragments, 2 core flakes, scrapers, 1 blade made into an awl, 3 microliths, 1 retouched blade and 1 large obliquely blunted blade. The industry is suggestive of large scale tool manufacture and might be a temporary chipping floor, hence the numbers of cores and unretouched blades. Uncritical collection may have severely distorted the relative proportions of artifacts. If we assume that the site represents a settlement locale for the exploitation of the surrounding area, an analysis of the site territory (Fig. 15) reveals a very similar situation to that described for the Lackford site. The site is in a similar situation, on a ridge between two tributaries of the river Lark, about ¼km from the nearest water source. The two-hour territory embraces areas of both closed and more open forest and the inferred economic strategy would be the same as that suggested for Lackford.

Kenny Hill T.L. 670.780 (general area)

One diagnostic obliquely blunted microlith, blunted down the left hand side and with a small shoulder, was associated with a small industry comprising microblade cores, unretouched blades and scrapers and debitage. Tranchet axes came from the same general vicinity. The artifacts are now lost or mixed with other collections. Site catchment analysis (Fig. 16) shows that the site is situated on the fen edge/forest ecotone. Approximately 40% of the one- and two-hour territory consists of fenland, the rest being light mixed pine and deciduous forest. The site is situated on a sandy hill providing good views of game movements and might be compatible with a winter occupation.

Lakenheath T.L. 725.825 (Sturge 1912; Jacobi 1976)

From the large amount of material derived from surface collections this is an obvious occupation site. Two distinct groups of material occur: a patinated group with a high proportion of simple microlith shapes, and an unpatinated group dominated by narrow rods and scalene triangles. This might indicate either two distinct occupations of the site at different periods or the production of the simpler microlith forms in a later industry. In this area the soil profile has been changing from a calcareous brown earth to an acid podsol so that the differential degree of patination might have chronological significance. The patinated industry is quite similar to those at Shippea Hill and Wangford, Oat Hill, and so might well be given a later date. In the absence of any stratigraphic or other chronological controls it is not possible to provide any firm statement as to the relative ages of the patinated and unpatinated groups. Here it is tentatively assumed that there may have been two separate occupations of the site, one towards the end of the earlier Mesolithic and one in the later Mesolithic, on the basis of the differential patination, and the quantitatively very large surface collections that have been derived from this area, most of which are in private collections or have been lost.

Site catchment analysis reveals a situation similar to that at Kenny Hill but with a smaller area of the fen basin within the two-hour territory (Fig. 17). Jacobi (1976) analyzed a sample of microliths from this site (see Table 2 and Fig. 18).

Wangford T.L. 746.834 (Clark 1932)

A series of flints with lustrous green patination came from this general area, including cores and waste flakes, shouldered points and obliquely blunted blades. Fig. 19 shows a section through the general area. The precise location of the site is uncertain and quite conceivably the finds could have come from the Lakenheath area (Jacobi, personal communication). The general area is in a typical fen edge ecotone situation.

Honey Hill T.L. 443.881 (general area)

Honey Hill is an 'island' in the central area of the fen basin where a number of Mesolithic finds have been made, including early broad blade microlithic forms. Once again the total number of finds is very restricted and it would be unwise to place too much emphasis upon them. Fig. 20 shows the site catchment analysis.

Later Mesolithic Sites 6,800-3,500 b.c.
Wangford T.L. 746-834 (general area)

The later unpatinated series at this site is dominated by narrow scalene triangles, rods blunted down one or two sides, rhomboids, lunates, boat and pear shaped microtranchet microliths. A number of earlier forms such as obliquely blunted points occur in the industry.

Lakenheath T.L. 725.825 (general area)(see above, page 39)

A flake and blade industry with microliths comes from the same general area as the earlier patinated series. Table 2 shows an analysis of microlith classes and Fig. 21 their proportional representation.

Wangford, Oat Hill T.L. 744.834

A small excavation at this extensive site was carried out in 1972 producing a valuable spatial analysis of worked flints (Figs. 22, 23). A notable concentration of flints correlating with areas of burnt flint and subsoil marked a hearth area. The flint industry is comparable in size with that from the Lackford site. Numbers of recognizable tool classes, likewise, were relatively small. Microburins resulting from the notch and break technique of microlith manufacture are scattered around the periphery of the main flint concentration whereas most scrapers and microliths exhibit a strong tendency to cluster within, and immediately adjacent to, the hearth area. There is an approximately equal spatial decline in flint debris from the central hearth in all directions but with possible secondary working areas to the north and west. Most flintwork is concentrated within a 40m square. Brinch Petersen (1971) has recently argued that "ghost structures" may be indicated by a grid analysis of the distribution and density of artifacts which may be used to define crudely the units of a structure. This is a brave attempt to add a social dimension to what must otherwise remain an uninterpretable mass of arti-facts. If we apply Naroll's (1962) formula and that deduced by Weissner (1974) from a study of ! Kung occupation sites we may tentatively assign a population of four to eight people to the Oat Hill site, a minimal or slightly extended familial group.

A number of activity areas may be tentatively distinguished. There is a cooking/roasting hearth area 5m^2. Hide or vegetable processing may have taken place immediately beside the hearth to the north, hence the high scraper density. Microlith manufacture may have taken place in the south-west of the area, where the microburin concentrations are found. It is obvious that this excavated area is only a small portion of much more extensive site.

The settlement is positioned on a low ridge of sandy subsoil in the general area we have delimited as the fen edge ecotone. 20% of the two-hour terri-tory consists of fen, the rest being "dry" oak-hazel deciduous forest asso-ciations (Fig. 25).

Lackford T.L. 782-712

Here a late industry postdates that associated with the windbreak structure. Todd (1947) recorded a single narrow rod and a small triangle identical to examples from Peacock's Farm from blown sand above the earlier structure. These can be associated with a number of surface finds from the same general area.

Shippea Hill T.L. 636-847 (Clark, Clifford and Godwin 1934, Clark 1955)

A microlithic industry was found scattered on a sand ridge in the centre of the fens extending into a horizontal scatter in the lower peat. Cutting A of the 1934 excavations revealed a Mesolithic core in a black sticky band running through the peat. No material was discovered below this band, which had a high sand content and possibly represents a phase in which the natural vegetation was disturbed and surface water run-off carried sand and silt from the surface of the sand deposit on which the occupation was centered into surrounding peat areas. No diagnostic Mesolithic material was recovered from Cutting B. Cuttings C and D yielded greater quantities of material in-cluding narrow flakes, cores with narrow flaking scars, a core dressing flake, 6 complete and fragmentary microliths, 2 microburins and a possible burin.

The industry occupies a position late in pollen zone VIc. Birch and alder are well represented in the pollen diagrams with oak, elm, lime and hazel, the last showing a decline possibly as a result of local clearance since hazel would be most likely to have colonized the sandy occupation area which would be constantly disturbed while not being tolerant of surrounding marshy areas. Pollen from elm, oak and lime are more likely to be representative of the regional vegetative situation whereas that of hazel and alder more localised conditions. This and the macroscopic evidence discussed by Godwin (1934) indicate areas of deciduous forest on the higher fen 'islands' adjacent to the site and fringing fen carr on the edge of the sand ridge. The Mesolithic horizon is bracketed by the radiocarbon dates 5650±150 (Q587) and 4735±150 (Q586) b.c.

Surface finds were analyzed by Clark (1955). Below is an analysis of the industry derived from both the excavations and the surface collections.

Cores: 27 single platform (15 converted into core scrapers)
27 double platform (19 converted into core scrapers)
3 treble platform
1 quadruple platform
1 converted into an angle burin

Flakes: considerable quantities of narrow pointed forms

Microliths: 72, 12 from excavations
23 obliquely blunted points
12 points with battered backs (straight and convex)
3 points with basal retouch
a few triangular, crescentic and quadrangular microliths
17 microburins
5 burins
2 awls
6 retouched flakes

The location and restricted size of the site suggests only a temporary occupation of short duration. The combined thickness of occupation material, as Clark noted, is only a few inches out of over 20 ft of deposits. The potential area for settlement at Shippea Hill, that is, the surface of the sand ridge, is only 80m^2, an area which might support 4-6 minimal social units (2 adults adn 2 children) or 16-24 people. Site catchment analysis (Fig. 25) shows that 98% of the one-hour territory and 80% of the two-hour territory consists of fenland. The most realistic interpretation would be a seasonally occupied summer site possibly used for no more than a few days.

The presence of cores, core rejuvenation flakes and microburins indicates tool manufacture upon the site. The cores passed through more than one phase of use, a very high proportion being converted into core scrapers. The site is approximately 7 km from the nearest flint source and it is evident that flint must have been a scarce and valued raw material in the fens, hence the economy of usage exhibited at Shippea Hill and the small absolute quantity of flint in the assemblage and the high proportion of tools to debitage, in contrast with the situation we find in the Breckland zone.

Plantation Farm (Clark 1932) T.L. 637-847

A possibly contemporaneous site existed on an adjacent sand ridge about 300 yards to the south-west on the other side of a now extinct river course. A boring through the lower peat brought up one typical Mesolithic primary flake. Surface collection from the sand ridge produced waste flakes, cores obliquely blunted points and rod microliths.

Little Fen Drove, Swaffham T.L. 551-662

Surface collections from a rounded rise approximately 0.50 m higher than the adjacent fenland illustrate the critical importance of micro-topography for settlement location. The site was originally adjacent to an old river course; 60% of the one-hour territory (fig. 26) consists of fenland. The site is within ecotone and the two-hour territory includes areas of "wet" deciduous forest. As at Shippea Hill the area for settlement is restricted and is suggestive of a short lived occupation. The industry includes 28 microblade cores, 4 end of blade scrapers and 15 microliths—rods, triangles, obliquely blunted points and 1 Horsham point. Four tranchet axes come from the surrounding area.

Sandhills Site T.L. 535-679

Surface collection of a geometric industry was made from a low elliptical rise about 2.50 m above the surrounding fenland with a virtually identical catchment to the Little Fen Drove site.

Wilde Street, Beck Row. T.L. 704.794

The material from this site includes 11 microblade cores, 12 unretouched flakes and blades, 10 scrapers, 3 gravers, 9 non-geometric microliths and 3 microburins. This small surface collection is possibly representative of a much larger industry. The site is situated on a minor elevation above the surrounding fenland. The site is in a fen edge ecotone situation (Fig. 27).

King's site, Beck Row. T.L. 704.795

This site has a very large industry (8000 objects) with a high proportion of debitage, backed blades, utilised flakes, cores, scrapers and burins. The industry includes 19 scrapers, 19 gravers, 45 spalls, 4 large flake scrapers, 20 retouched blades, 13 truncated blades, 18 microliths and 13 microburins. The large number of spalls from burins manufacture may indicate the importance of piercing tools for hide, bone and antler working. This supports our economic model, which suggested that in this area we might expect to find large sites occupied during the autumn. If burins were primarily associated with antler working then, as red deer antler is in prime condition during the autumn, we might expect sites occupied during this season to have a large proportion of burins and other tools associated with animal exploitation such as hide scrapers (Clark 1972).

Coles (1965) incorrectly assigns this site to a Late-glacial occupation, calling it 'The Mildenhall site', but it is obvious from an analysis of the flint industry that it is of later Mesolithic date. A series of banana-shaped hollows, interpreted as house structures, were reported from the site but these are probably intrusive and of Bronze Age date (Jacobi, personal communication). The site catchment is basically similar to that of the Wilde Street site (Fig. 27).

Other sites, possibly late

London Bottom, Icklingham (Sturge 1912) T.L. 774-737 (general area)

A mixed Mesolithic/Neolithic industry was discovered in an area of river gravels 30-40 ft wide and 300 yards long, possibly extending further along the valley bottom. Site catchment analysis (Fig. 28) indicates use of areas of "damp" and "dry" deciduous woodland.

Icklingham Plains T.L. 760-735 (general area)

A large flint scatter including diagnostic narrow blade microlith forms occurs throughout the general area of this broad river valley. A number of isolated surface collections are recorded in the Cambridge Museum but as yet no certain occupation site is known.

Brandon T.L. 790-860 (general area)

Again quantities of material are limited and include six geometric microliths, an awl, a few microburins and unretouched blades and flakes.

Gamlingay T.L. 233-515

A number of objects were found in the inside of the moat at Dutter's End including a tranchet axe, a microblade core, 9 flakes, 1 plunging flake, 1 microlith, 1 fragment of a bifacial point and 2 natural stones, possibly hammerstones. Site catchment analysis (Fig. 29) indicates that the site was positioned in order to exploit the wet deciduous forest zone and in this respect is unique within the Cambridge region.

Sahara Site, Kenny Hill T.L. 732-831

A large flake and blade industry comes from this general area. The site is situated upon a sandy ridge within the fen edge ecotone.

Hallard's Fen Hightown Drove, Burwell T.L. 572-578

The site is positioned upon a small area of higher ground surrounded by fenland in a classic fen edge position with 40% of the one-hour territory consisting of fenland (Fig. 30). The material includes 2 tranchet axes, 7 blades, 3 microblade cores, 1 scraper, 1 microlith and a number of unretouched flakes.

Fen Ditton T.L. 478.601 (Marr, King and Lethbridge 1923)

Material from this site includes 22 microlithic blade cores, 11 unretouched flakes, 4 scrapers, 2 gravers, 1 tranchet axe, 2 awls, 1 microburin, 4 microliths and debitage. It may represent a temporary camp site as the industry is quantitatively very small. The site is on a ridge of high ground near to the Cam. Fen comprises only 10% of the one-hour territory and 15% of the two-hour territory (Fig. 31). The majority of the two-hour territory would embrace areas of "damp" deciduous forest.

CHAPTER VI

A CONSIDERATION OF THE PREDICTED PATTERNS OF SETTLEMENT AND
SUBSISTENCE IN RELATION TO THE SUBSTANTIVE EVIDENCE.

Having made a survey of the available material an attempt will be made
to relate this to the models and hypotheses made in the earlier sections of this
work. Map F shows the location of Mesolithic sites in the Cambridge region.
The distribution map clearly shows continuity in the preferred settlement location
between Early and Late Mesolithic assemblages, often with the same site location
as at Lackford, Lakenheath and Wangford being occupied or sites in very similar
locations.

On a priori grounds we might expect that population would rise in relation
to the higher post glacial values of vegetative productivity and more stable animal
biomass densities (cf.Zubrow 1971; 1975). In fact we do not have any evidence
of an increase in population, based on site density, unless we include those of
indeterminate date, in which case there is a 60% increase. The total number
of sites is so small that this may not be significant anyway, given sampling
biases.

The sites have been tentatively divided into two classes, large sites and
small sites, based on numbers of artifacts and the spatial extent of the artifact
scatter. All the larger sites occur in the Breckland area along with some
smaller satellite extraction (?) camps. Smaller sites occur in the fen basin[8]
and in the 'damp' deciduous forest zones. It is suggested that the larger sites
might result from autumnal gatherings of people for hazel nut and perhaps
bracken root collection, processing and storage and for social purposes. The
expectation that we might find large numbers of sites in the fen basin, occupied
during the summer months with possibly a more dispersed population, has not
been fulfilled. This might be due to sampling factors and the heavy rate of
post Mesolithic deposition of sediments that has taken place. The absence of
evidence for extensive occupation from the fen 'islands' is particularly interesting and this might relate to their low exploitative potential compared with a
purely fenland position. The tranchet axe distribution Map E confirms this
picture. The small size and limited number of sites utilizing the "damp"
deciduous forest zone (Gamlingay and Fen Ditton) would seem to support the
proposition that these might be spring/summer locational choices with a high
degree of population dispersal.

There is a significant lack of Mesolithic material from the "damp" deciduous forest zone and central regions of the fen basin. The Gamlingay site
might however indicate that this may be partially due to sampling problems.
The M11 survey (Browne 1972) produced isolated material from a number of
locations which would have been in the "damp" deciduous forest zone.

Chi-square tests were performed in order to determine whether or not the Mesolithic sites could be correlated with any of the five ecological zones (see Maps C and F). The Chi ^{2} statistic was very significant as the expected number of sites to be found within the fen edge ecotone was only 2.7 while the observed number was 19. This confirms our proposition that the fen edge ecotone might be the most productive region and therefore the most preferred area for settlement, especially the "dry" deciduous forest and fenland ecotone situation. Here most sites are located on sandy ridges affording a dry subsoil which provided a suitable base for occupation and views of game movements. The high density of settlement in the Breckland/fen edge region indicates the possibility that environmental manipulation of the type indicated in Chapter IV (vi) may have taken place.

The site catchment analyses indicate the critical importance of fen deposits to site location. Only Lackford, Cavenham and London Bottom, Gamlingay and Icklingham have virtually no fen resources within the two-hour territory. Conversely very few sites depend entirely upon fen resources. The emphasis is clearly upon integration of two or more ecological zones. In the absence of any faunal data and bearing in mind the biased nature if the flint industries, the problem of seasonality and site distribution cannot be investigated further without tautology.

A comparative consideration of the lithic assemblages cannot be at all rigorous as most of the material consists of largely uncontrolled surface collections. The derivation of evidence relating to seasonality from lithic material is fraught with difficulties since precise functions are difficult to assign in the absence of detailed studies of use-wear patterns. Since red deer antlers are present in autumn and winter one might expect burins, if associated with antler working, to be relatively more important during these seasons (Clarke 1972: 29). In terms of our model we should expect burins to be most common on sites in the fen edge ecotone and in the 'dry' deciduous forest zones and the data would seem to confirm this (King's site, Beck Row). On the other hand Shippea Hill, which we have tentatively attributed to a summer occupation, has comparatively few burins.

A pattern of seasonal movements of the base camp coupled with sequential fission and fusion of social units would seem to be indicated by the distribution of sites within the Cambridge region and model 2 (Fig. 11) would seem most appropriate. The major axis of movement would seem to be from the fen basin to the dry deciduous forest zone in the north-east of the Cambridge region with the proposed summer sites at one end of the axis (the fen basin) and large seasonal aggregations of the autumn occupation at the other and with spring/winter sites positioned in the intermediate region—the fen edge ecotone. Such a pattern would not be rigid but would be flexible enough to repond to seasonal and/or annual resource fluctuations. In the long run regularities in site location ought to be observed, and it is these site positions that the model utilized here attempts to demonstrate. The base camps for various seasons are expected to have been of different sizes reflecting patterns of aggregation and dispersal of the population, and hence we should have fewer large summer and spring sites than autumn/winter locations. This may be the reason, aggravated by sampling considerations, why as yet no large occupation locale has been found within the fen basin.

CHAPTER VII

THE MESOLITHIC-NEOLITHIC TRANSITION

Recent publications have questioned the validity of the blanket terms "Mesolithic" and "Neolithic" as an apt way of describing particular forms of material culture, subsistence or settlement patterns. Such a terminology may ossify research and obscure rather than aid any evaluation of cultural change. It has been argued (Higgs and Jarman 1972) that we should think in terms of energy cost thresholds in relation to domestication, or the use of a characteristic lithic technology, rather than in the crude terms of a presence/absence perspective.

Agricultural systems may be considered as being modified ecosystems of a rather specialized type, usually with a low diversity index compared with natural ecosystems (Harris 1972). The agricultural utilization of a ecosystem may take place by processes of manipulation rather than direct transformation, especially in the initial stages of the introduction of such an economy. Particular elements may be altered without fundamentally changing the overall structure of the ecosystem. Certain preferred domestic species may be substituted for wild ones occupying equivalent ecological niches. The most important implication of this is that it concentrates usable productivity, increasing edible yield per unit area of land. In Chapter 4 (vi) suggestions were made relating to Mesolithic subsistence and environmental manipulation. We would expect that, in view of the special nature of the resources of the fen basin, in many areas between 3,500 and 2,00 B.C. an economy based upon hunting and gathering may have persisted. Such an economy may have integrated agricultural activities at specific times and places within the annual circuit. The earliest known Neolithic site in the Cambridge region is at Shippea Hill (Clarke, Godwin and Clifford 1935; Clarke and Godwin 1962). The pottery is technically of high quality, undecorated, with simple rolled over or beaded rims. The sherds extended over the sand ridge with a scatter in the lower peat. The continuity of occupation above the Mesolithic layers is significant. This might indicate the continuation of an essentially Mesolithic economic strategy and the use of similar exploitative processes. The site would certainly seem to be unsuited to anything but a temporary occupation and might be unlikely to support a fully fledged agricultural regime. The 5 km site territory consists entirely of wet fen vegetation.

Neolithic projectile points cluster in precisely those ecological zones that in the Mesolithic we have suggested would have been in preferential use for big game hunting—the fen edge ecotone and the 'dry' deciduous forest zone (Table 4, Map J). Chi-square tests confirmed the non-random distribution of Neolithic projectile points and their extremely selective clustering on the sandy Breckland soils (see Table 3) and in the 'dry' deciduous forest and fen-edge ecotone.

Both the total Neolithic polished axe distribution and that of the ground-stone axes taken alone was equivalent (Tables 3 and 4). The chi-square statistic was well above the 0.001% significance level, invalidating the null hypothesis that the axes were randomly distributed. There are comparatively few axes on the heavy boulder clay soils and a far greater concentration is found on the fen basin soils and on the sandy Breckland soils. There were approxi - mately the numbers we would expect on the rendzina/loam soils which, because of their high fertility, we might expect to have been associated primarily with agricultural activities such as land clearance[9]. In relation to ecological zones the Neolithic axes selectively clustered in the fen-edge ecotone and in the 'dry' deciduous forest area, repeating the distribution pattern of the Mesolithic tranchet axes. The only major difference appears to be an increase in the absolute numbers of artifacts. Significantly, however, there are very few tranchet axes on the rendzina/terrace loam soils with their high agricultural potential and roughly the number of Neolithic polished flint and groundstone axes we would expect on these soils, assuming a random distribution. The overall distribution of the Neolithic axes, when compared with the Mesolithic tranchet axes, indicates utilization of a wider range of both soil types and ecological zones during the Neolithic. This may relate to a gradual broadening of the economy to include agricultural activities.

Earlier Neolithic sites should repeat the locational tendencies postulated for the Mesolithic period, if the economic strategy was similar as is suggested here. Later sites might reflect radically different locational 'pulls' in relation to ecological zones and soil types and as a result of changing environmental conditions (see below). A major difficulty, since we lack radiocarbon dates or significant pottery finds from many of the sites on which we might build reliable regional typologies, is to distinquish early and later sites. Where evidence permits, largely using arrow-head types, an attempt has been made (Map K). Failure to achieve temporal control critically affects any attempt to test the hypotheses put forward in this chapter. The large number of sites re-covered by the M II survey (Map L) strongly suggests (a) that those sites we do have in other areas represent a minimal sample, and (b) that a far wider range of environments was used than we might previously have expected was utilized. Sites cluster in the 'dry' deciduous forest zone and the fen edge ecotone repeating the Mesolithic pattern. Sites were preferentially located upon the productive loam/rendzina soils and on the sandy Breckland soils (Tables 3 and 4).

The elm decline, represented in the pollen diagrams at Shippea Hill, occurs at the base of the Neolithic layers. Godwin interprets the pollen curves as an indication of initial forest clearance. The grass curve is noticeably low and may not provide unequivocal evidence of forest clearance, except on a small scale. There is no supporting evidence whatsoever to suggest cereal cultivation. Sims (1973) interprets the elm decline at Hockham Mere as marking a threshold point when large scale and relatively permanent slash and burn agriculture as opposed to husbandry begins, but this would seem to be a largely unsupported assumption. No cereals have been recorded from Shippea Hill. The only fau-nal remains are of red deer, pig, ox and sheep. The occurence of domesti-cates at Shippea Hill would be wholly compatible with a summer occupation integrated within a pattern of seasonal movement, at least initially. This would

48

be a means of producing a greater measure of stability in the socioeconomic system. Darby (1940) documents the unique productivity of the fen basin as a source of cattle fodder in the Middle Ages. Cattle were seasonally driven along drove-ways in early summer into the fens in order to feed in the rich vegetation. In the thirteenth century an acre of meadowland was deemed to be worth twice or three times as much as arable land. The numerous cattle bones discovered at the recently excavated double interrupted ditched enclosure at Great Wilbraham, located in a fen edge situation, acts as some measure of support for this argument. The only really significant change with the advent of the Neolithic would seem to be the addition of pottery to the material culture assemblage; the ceramic 'dye' making these essentially hunter-fisher-gatherer sites archeologically more visible. Radiocarbon dates obtained from charcoal and peat samples at Shippea Hill indicate that the 'Neolithic' layers can be dated to around 3300 b.c.

These early 'Neolithic' groups may represent a climax situation embodying a culmination of behavioural possibilities under specific exploitative premisses. We would expect an extemely efficient utilization of energy and a population size near local saturation. Adopting systems terminology we may charcterize this as a state of metastable equilibrium. The situation is only likely to remain stable in the absence of a suitable catalyst, being so delicately adjusted to the external natural and social environment—a threshold state preceding sudden change. A comparatively minor change in the controlling variables would be likely to result in rapid sociocultural change. It is obvious that any decrease in resource availability would have a drastic impact upon the functioning of pre-existing systems. A situation of imbalance would be created without a drastic decline of population: the only solution would be to adjust both settlement and subsistence systems in order to cope with the new exigencies.

The buttery clay, seen clearly in the stratigraphy, at Shippea Hill and other fenland sites, was laid down as a result of an extensive marine transgression occurring between 2,700 and 2,300 b.c. reaching its maximum extent around 2,400 b.c. In many areas, especially in the central regions of the fen basin, the sea covered extensive areas of peat resulting in the classic sequence described by Clark (1934) of (i) lower peat, (ii) buttery clay, (iii) upper peat. We have radiocarbon dates of around 2,400 b.c. for wood in the basal peat layers at Adventurer's Fen (Godwin and Willis 1961). At sites in Wicken Fen, Reach Fen and at Upware pollen analyses show that forest peat was succeeded by Cladium sedge peat formed under much wetter conditions. This wet period corresponds with the deposition of buttery clay further seaward. A rise in sea level may have been an important factor stimulating changes in subsistence in strategy towards a fully fledged agricultural regime in the Cambridge region.

Two important variables seem to have contributed to the differences between the Mesolithic and early Neolithic sites in the Cambridge region and the later Neolithic period. Firstly, there seems to have been a major population increase. We might tentatively infer this from the number of sites and their wider spatial dispersion (Map K). Secondly, the environment had, in terms of resource potential, drastically deteriorated. An important concomitant of marine incursion would be a displacement of population and a disruption of traditional seasonal population movements adjusted to resource availability. The pressures to augment food supplies would call for an efficiency response and would tend to select for technologies and organizational structures that would maximize or extend the capabilities of the labour supply in Athens' (1977) terms. Social systems will become more differentiated and their internal and external articulation will become more complex. Signs of such a change can be seen in the development of large enclosure sites such as those at Great Wilbraham, Melbourn and possibly Hurst Fen with its unexplained ditch system (Clark 1960), in the use of elaborate exchange items such as the three jadeite axes documented from the region, in certain pottery types (Frere 1943) and in complex funerary practices (Briscoe 1957).

CHAPTER VIII

CONCLUSIONS

The present archaeological material is pitifully inadequate to test in any meaningful way any of the theoretical models proposed in the discussion, and therefore the tone of this monograph must remain largely speculative. The efficient execution of the research objectives that have been set out above would clearly require a long term research design adopting formalized probability sampling procedures in order reliably to test our erected models and hypotheses so that we can arrive at explanations for sociocultural phenomena. This was not possible within the scope of the present study. The only reliable survey we have is the transect approximately 200ft wide and 12 miles long [10] along the M11 route in the south-west of the region. This produced some Mesolithic material including a previously unrecorded tranchet axe. Unfortunately we cannot interpolate from this sample to the rest of the region. As Mueller (1974) has indicated, the rights of way laid out by engineers do not conform to sampling theory nor are they totally random as they tend to follow easily traversable terrain and do not represent all or most of the environmental diversity within a region.

With the increasing destruction of the peat areas due to agricultural activities and drainage systems, we need to locate occupation locales with good chances of preservation so that faunal and floral data may be obtained. This is not feasible in the Breckland region owing to the acid nature of the subsoil. An investigation of fenland microtopography would indicate the most likely areas for settlement which could then be further investigated.

Binford (1965), Clarke (1968; 1972a), Hill (1972) and others have emphasized the need for a hypothetico-deductive approach in archaeological studies. We isolate a series of problems, set up a series of models proposing solutions to these problems and draw hypotheses and test implications. We then look at the relevant data in order to confirm of falsify our theoretical position. Merton (1957: 9) and Binford (1977), in an archaeological context, have directed attention towards the need to bridge the gap between theories in the strict sense and raw empiricism with theories of the middle range. Middle range theory consists of generalized propositions and orientations towards data, suggesting the types of variables which our theories must somehow try to take into account. Middle range theory may be examined empirically but also must have sufficient generality to be incorporated into even broader generalizations. It provides a useful bridge between descriptive factual studies and the formulation of rigorous, parsimonious theoretical systems. The latter can only be achieved as the end result of a protracted period of research involving the building, manipulation and refinement of numerous theories and models on a more modest scale. If this piece of research has done little more, it has isolated a set of problems, models, hypotheses and test implications. In the absence of any large body

51

of reliable evidence it simply is not possible to go much further. The next step would be to survey systematically the entire area, setting up a probabalistic sampling scheme which could be stratified on the basis of our hypothesized ecological zones and following this a series of selective research excavations. The Cambridge region offers much potential for a detailed investigation of the dynamics of sociocultural change. Sadly, this potential is largely unrealized and with the increasing scale and intensity of agricultural disturbance, particularly in the fen basin, the opportunity may soon be lost altogether.

NOTES

1. Extensive reindeer culls in the spring are not, perhaps, so probable because of the problem of meat storage with the climate becoming warmer during the summer months.

2. Whether or not Bracken formed an extensive part of the diet, of indeed made any contribution to it, is a controversial point in view of the lack of any direct evidence. However, as there is very little evidence for the use of any other plant foods in the Mesolithic, apart from hazel, this point cannot be disproved on negative evidence alone (see Clark 1972 for a list of other possible plant food sources found at Star Carr). Godwin (1975: 91-2) suggests that the dense Atlantic lime/oak forest would have been unfavourable to the development of large areas of bracken growth because it requires a high light intensity and therefore would only become common with the advent of large scale forest clearance. On the other hand we might expect a far greater bracken ground cover in areas of less dense 'dry' deciduous forest as postulated in this paper which would afford greater possibilities for exploitation, especially if coupled with some form of environmental manipulation as is suggested in Chapter IV, section vi.

3. The spatial extent of the lower peat development is quite uncertain from the literature. The area of fen development was certainly considerably smaller than that of the medieval fenland. Extensive stratigraphic studies are clearly required before we can be sure how much peat development there was in the early Post-glacial period.

4. Godwin (1978; 611) suggests that elk may have persisted in the fenland area until towards the end of the Bronze Age. This suggestion is made on the basis of what are described as 'elk droppings' found in the sphagnum peat between the top of the fen clay and the overlying shell marl at Ugg Mere, Huntingdonshire, with a date of 1310-100 b.c. Lacking any other evidence whatsoever for the presence of elk in England at such a late date, either the identification of the droppings or the radiocarbon date would appear to be suspect.

5. This also indicates that tranchet axes were probably not used as exchange items.

6. At the Wawcott site, Carter (1976) demonstrates a trend towards the exploitative pattern concentrating on Bos in the later occupations with red deer, roe deer and pig becoming less important. He suggests that this might be associated with the abandonment of marsh and riverine areas as hunting grounds in favour of the deciduous forest. (Carter, H. H., 1976. 'Fauna of an area of Mesolithic occupation in the Kennet valley considered in relation to contemporary eating habits', Berkshire Archaeological Journal Vol. 68, pp. 1-3).

7. A rise in the absolute number of sites does not provide unequivocal evidence of population rise since we need to be quite certain of their functional significance whether they be true living sites or simply temporary camps or specialized extraction camps.

8. Honey Hill, Shippea Hill, Plantation Farm, Little Fen Drove, Sandhills site, Gamlingay, Sahara site, Fen Ditton, Hallard's Fen, Hightown Drove.

9. The association of Neolithic groundstone axes and some form of exchange has, of course, long been recognized. A skull of an aurochs, with a smashed-in frontal bone, from Burwell Fen was found in association with a Neolithic polished axe, perhaps indicating their use as hunting implements (Godwin 1978: 167).

10. Since this research was completed a broad regional survey of the fenland has begun (Hall 1977). Four additional Mesolithic surface flint scatters have been located, all on low sandy rises in the peat, a further indication of the preferential utilization of dry sandy soils and the critical import-ance of fenland microtopography for settlement location. One quite exten-sive site is located on a large area of sandy subsoil to the north of Shippea Hill, the smaller sites being at Manea, Soham and Isleham (Hall, personal communication).

REFERENCES

Ahlén, O., 1975. 'Winter habitats of Moose and Deer in relation to land use in Scandinavia', Viltrevy 9(3):45-192.

Aleksiuk, M. and Cowan, I. McT., 1969. 'Aspects of seasonal energy expenditure in the beaver (Castor canadensis Kuhl) at the Northern limits of its distribution', Canadian Journal of Zoology 47(4):471-481.

Athens, J. S., 1977. 'Theory building and the study of evolutionary process in complex societies' in L. R. Binford (ed.), For Theory Building in Archaeology, pp. 353-384. Academic Press, London.

Bannikov, A. G., 1970. 'Moose in the U.S.S.R. and its exploitation', Riistatieteelisia Julkaisuga (1970):273-276.

Ballenberghe, V. V. and Peek, J. M., 1971. 'Radiotelemetry studies of Moose in North-eastern Minnesota', Journal of Wildlife Management, 35(1):63-71.

Bay-Petersen, J. L., 1978. 'Animal exploitation in Mesolithic Denmark' in P. Mellars (ed.), The Early Post-glacial Settlement of Northern Europe, pp. 115-146. Duckworth, London.

Binford, L. R., 1962. 'Archaeology as Anthropology', American Antiquity, 28 (2):217-225.

Binford, L. R., 1964. 'A consideration of archaeological research design', American Antiquity, 29(4):425-441.

Binford, L. R., 1965. 'Archaeological systematics and the study of culture process', American Antiquity, 31(2):203-210.

Binford, L. R., 1977. 'General introduction' in L. R. Binford (ed.), For Theory Building in Archaeology, pp. 1-10. Academic Press, London.

Birdsell, J. B., 1957. 'Some Population problems involving Pleistocene man', Cold Spring Harbour Symposium on Quantative Biology, Vol. XXII: 47-69.

Birks, H. J. B., Deacon, J. and Peglar, S., 1975. 'Pollen maps for the British Isles 5000 years ago', Proceedings of the Royal Society of London, Ser. B, 189:87-105.

Brinch Petersen, E., 1971. 'Svaerdborg II: A Maglemose hut from Svaerdborg bog, Zealand, Denmark', Acta Archaeologica, Vol. 42:43-77.

Briscoe, G., 1957. 'Swales tumulus; a combined Neolithic A and Bronze Age barrow at Worlington, Suffolk', Proc. Cambridge Antiquarian Society L:101-112.

Browne, D. M., 1972. 'The MII Survey, Unpublished manuscript, Cambridge University.

Butzer, K. W., 1971. Environment and Archaeology, Aldine, Chicago (2nd edition).

Campbell, J. B., 1977. The Upper Palaeolithic of Britain, Clarendon Press, Oxford.

Clark, J. G. D., 1932. The Mesolithic Age in Britain, Cambridge University Press, London.

Clark, J. G. D., 1936. The Mesolithic Settlement of Northern Europe, Cambridge University Press, Cambridge.

Clark, J. G. D., 1938. 'The archaeology of the Cambridge region', in H. C. Darby (ed.), The Cambridge Region, pp. 80-98. Cambridge.

Clark, J. G. D., 1952. Prehistoric Europe: The Economic Basis, Methuen, London.

Clark, J. G. D., 1954. Star Carr, Cambridge University Press, Cambridge.

Clark, J. G. D., 1955. 'A microlithic industry from the Cambridgeshire Fenland and other industries of Sauveterrian affinities from Britain', Proc. Prehist. Soc., 21:3-21.

Clark, J. G. D., 1968. 'The economic impact of the change from late glacial to post glacial conditions in Northern Europe', VII International Congress of Anth. and Eth. Sciences, Vol. III:241-244.

Clark, J. G. D., 1972. 'Star Carr: a case study in bioarchaeology', Allison Wesley Module in Anthropology, No. 10.

Clark, J. G. D., 1975. The Earlier Stone Age Settlement of Scandinavia, Cambridge University Press, Cambridge.

Clark, J. G. D., Godwin, H. and Clifford, M. H., 1934. 'Report on recent excavations at Peacock's Farm, Shippea Hill, Cambridgeshire', Antiquaries Journal, XV:284-319.

Clark, J. G. D. and Godwin, H., 1962. 'The Neolithic in the Cambridgeshire Fens', Antiquity, XXXVI:10-23.

Clark, J. G. D., Higgs, E. S. and Longworth, I. H., 1960. 'Excavations at the Neolithic site at Hurst Fen, Mildenhall, Suffolk', Proc. Prehist. Society:202-245.

Clarke, D. L., 1968. Analytical Archaeology, Methuen, London.

Clarke, D. L., 1972a. 'Models and paradigms in contemporary archaeology' in D. L. Clarke (ed.), Models in Archaeology, Methuen, London.

Clarke, D. L., 1972b. 'A provisional model of an Iron Age society and its settlement system' in D. L. Clarke (ed.), Models in Archaeology, Methuen, London.

Clarke, D. L., 1976. 'Mesolithic Europe: The economic basis?' in G. de G. Sieveking, I. H. Longworth and K. E. Wilson (eds.), Problems in Economic and Social Archaeology, pp. 449-481. Duckworth, London.

Clarke, R. R., 1960. <u>East Anglia</u>, Thames and Hudson, London.

Clarke, R. R., Macdonald, J. and Watt, A. S., 1938. 'The Breckland' in H. C. Darby (ed.), <u>The Cambridge Region,</u> pp. 208-230. Cambridge.

Coles, J. M., 1965. 'Archaeology of the Cambridge Region' in J. A. Steers (ed.) <u>The Cambridge Region,</u> pp. 112-125. Cambridge.

Cook, S. F. and Heizer, R. F., 1968. 'Relationships among houses, settlement areas and population in aboriginal California' in K. C. Chang (ed.), <u>Settlement Archaeology,</u> pp. 79-116. National Press, Palo Alto, California.

Cowan, I. McT., Hoar, W. S. and Hatter, J., 1950. 'The effect of forest succession upon the quantity and upon the nutritive values of woody plants used as food by Moose', <u>Canadian Journal of Research</u>, 28:249-271.

Cowgill, G. L., 1977. 'The trouble with significance tests and what we can do about it', <u>American Antiquity</u> 42(3):350-369.

Damas, D., 1968. 'The diversity of Eskimo societies' in R. B. Lee and I. De Vore (eds.) <u>Man The Hunter,</u> pp. 111-117. Aldine, Chicago.

Darby, H. C., 1940. <u>The Medieval Fenland</u>, Cambridge University Press, Cambridge.

Darling, F. F., 1969. <u>A Herd of Red Deer,</u> Oxford University Press, London.

Dergebøl, M., 1964. 'Some remarks on late and post-glacial vertebrate fauna and its ecological relations in Northern Europe', <u>Supplement to the Journal of Animal Ecology</u> 3:71-85.

Dergebøl, M. and Fredskild, B., 1970. 'The Urus (Bos primigenius Bojanus) and Neolithic domesticated cattle (Bos taurus domesticus Linne) in Denmark, <u>Kongl. Danske Vidensk. Selsk. Biol. Skr.</u> 17, 1. Copenhagen.

Dills, G. G., 1970. 'The effect of prescribed burning upon deer browse', <u>Journal of Wildlife Mangement</u>, 34(3):540-545.

Dimbleby, G. W., 1962. <u>The Development of British Heathlands and their Soils</u>, Oxford University Press, London.

Dimbleby, G. W., 1967. <u>Plants and Archaeology</u>, John Baker, London.

Driver, H. E., 1961. <u>Indians of North America</u>, University of Toronto Press, Toronto.

Edwards, L. and Wallace, H. F., 1927. <u>Hunting and Stalking the Deer</u>, Longmans, London.

Egorov, O. V., 1967. <u>Wild Ungulates of Yakutia</u>, Israel Program for Scientific Translations, Jerusalem.

Evans, J. D., 1975. <u>The Environment of Early Man in the British Isles</u>, Elek, London.

Farrow, E. P., 1915. 'The ecology of Breckland', <u>Journal of Ecology</u>, 3:211-229.

Flannery, K. V., 1967. 'Culture history versus culture process: a debate in American archaeology', <u>Scientific American</u> 217(2):119-122.

Flannery, K. V., 1968. 'Archaeological systems theory and early Meso-america' in B. J. Meggers (ed.), Anthropological Archaeology in the Americas, pp. 67-87, Brooklyn.

Fleming, A., 1972. 'The genesis of pastoralism in European prehistory', World Archaeology, 4(2):179-191.

Foley, R., 1977. 'Space and energy: a method for analysing habitat value and utilization in relation to archaeological sites' in D. L. Clarke (ed.) Spatial Archaeology, pp. 163-188. Academic Press, London.

Fowler, G., 1933. 'Fenland waterways, past and present, South level district, Part I.', Proc. Cambridge Antiquarian Society, 33:108-128.

Fox, C., 1923. The Archaeology of the Cambridge Region, Cambridge University Press, Cambridge.

Frere, D. H. S., 1943. 'A late Neolithic grooved ware site near to Cambridge', Antiquaries Journal (1943):34-41.

Goddard, J., 1970. 'Movements of moose in a heavily hunted region in Ontario', Journal of Wildlife Management, 34(2):439-445.

Godwin, H., 1944. 'The age and origin of the Breckland heaths of East Anglia', Nature, Vol. 154, No. 3896; 6-7.

Godwin, H., 1956. The History of the British Flora, Cambridge Univ. Press, Cambridge.

Godwin, H., 1975. The History of the British Flora, Cambridge (2nd edition).

Godwin, H., 1978. Fenland: Its Ancient Past and Uncertain Future, Cambridge University Press, Cambridge.

Godwin, H. and Clifford, M., 1935. 'Controlling factors in the formation of fen deposits', Journal of Ecology 23:509-535.

Godwin, H. and Tallantire, P. A., 1951. 'Studies in the post glacial history of British vegetation XII: Hockham Mere, Norfolk', Journal of Ecology 39:285-307.

Grzimek, B., 1970. Enzyklopädie des Tierreiches, Heinemann Verlag, Zurich.

Hall, D., 1977. Report to the Department of the Environment by the Cambridgeshire Archaeological Committee of work Completed by the Fenland Field Officer, Oct. 1976-Sept. 1977.

Hayden, B., 1972. 'Populations control amongst hunter-gatherers', World Archaeology, 4(2):205-221.

Hassan, F. A., 1975. 'The determination of the size, density and growth rate of hunting and gathering populations' in S. Polgar (ed.) Population, Ecology and Social Evolution, pp. 27-53. Mouton, Paris.

Hedrick, U. P., 1972 (ed.). Sturtevant's Edible Plants of the World, Dover, London.

Heptner, V. G., Nasimovic, A. A. and Bannikov, A. G., 1966. Die Säugetiere der Sowjetunien, Jena.

Higgs, E. S. and Shawcross, W., 1961. 'Excavation of a Bos primigenius at Loew's Farm, Littleport', Proceedings of the Cambridge Antiquarian Society, LIV:3-16.

Hill, J. N., 1972. 'The methodological debate in contemporary archaeology' in D. L. Clarke (ed.) Models in Archaeology, pp. 61-109. Methuen, London.

Hodge, C. A. H. and Seale, R. A., 1966. 'The Soils of the District Around Cambridge', Mem. Soil Survey, H.M.S.O. London.

Hosley, N. W., 1949. 'The moose and its ecology', U.S. Dept. of the Interior Wildlife Leaflet, 312.

Howes, F. N., 1948. Nuts: Their Production and Everyday Uses, Faber, London.

Innis, H. A., 1956. The Fur Trade in Canada: An Introduction to Economic History, University of Toronto Press, Toronto (revised edition).

Jacobi, R. M., 1973. 'The British Mesolithic' in S. K. Kozlowski (ed.) The Mesolithic in Europe, pp. 237-265. Warsaw.

Jacobi, R. M., 1976. Aspects of the Post Glacial Archaeology of England and Wales. Unpublished Ph.D. thesis, Cambridge University.

Jacobi, R. M., 1978a. 'Population and landscape in Mesolithic lowland Britain' in S. Limbrey and J. G. Evans (eds.) The Effect of Man on the Landscape: The Lowland Zone, pp. 75-85. C.B.A. Research Report 21.

Jacobi, R. M., 1978b. 'Northern England in the eighth millennium b.c.: an essay' in P. Mellars (ed.) The Early Post Glacial Settlement of Northern Europe, pp. 295-332. Duckworth, London.

Jacobi, R. M., Tallis, J. H., and Mellars, P. A., 1976. 'The Southern Pennine Mesolithic and the ecological record', Journal of Archaeological Science 3:207-20.

Jarman, M. R., 1972a. 'European deer economies and the advent of the Neolithic' in E. S. Higgs (ed.) Papers in Economic Prehistory, pp. 125-148. Cambridge University Press, Cambridge.

Jarman, M. R., 1972b. 'A territorial model for archaeology: a behavioural and geographical approach' in D. L. Clarke (ed.) Models in Archaeology, pp. 705-734. Methuen, London.

Jensen, P., 1968. 'Food selection of the Danish Red Deer (Cervus elephas L.) as determined by examination of the rumen content', Danish Review of Game Biology, 5(3):3-44.

Jochim, M. A., 1976. Hunter-Gatherer Subsistence and Settlement: A Predictive Model, Academic Press, London.

Lee, R. B., 1968. 'What hunters do for a living, or how to make out on scarce resources' in R. B. Lee and I. De Vore (eds.) Man The Hunter, pp. 30-48. Aldine, Chicago.

Liljegren, R. and Welinder, S. 'Pollen analytical dating of the skeleton of an aurochs', Geologiska Foreningens i Stockholm Forhandlingar 93: 662-72.

Lowe, V. P. W., 1966. 'Observations on the dispersal of red deer on Rhum' in P. A. Jewell and C. Loizos (eds.) Play, Exploration and Territory in Mammals, pp. 211-28.

Masefield, G. B., Wallis, M., Harrison, S. G. and Nicholson, B. E., 1971. The Oxford Book of Plant Foods, Oxford University Press, London.

Marr, J., King, W. and Lethbridge, T., 1923. 'An upper Palaeolithic site at Fen Ditton', Proc. Cambridge Antiquarian Society (1923):16-20.

McCullough, D. R., 1969. The Tule Elk, University of California Press, Berkeley.

Mellars, P. A., 1974. 'The Palaeolithic and Mesolithic' in C. A. Renfrew (ed.) British Prehistory: A New Outline, pp. 41-99. Duckworth, London.

Mellars, P. A., 1975. 'Ungulate Populations, economic patterns and the Mesolithic landscape' in J. G. Evans, S. Limbrey and H. Cleere (eds.) The Effect of Man on the Landscaee: The Highland Zone, pp. 49-56. Council for British Archaeology Research Report, II. London.

Mellars, P. A., 1976a. 'Settlement patterns and industrial variability in the British Mesolithic' in G. de G. Sieveking, I. H. Longworth and K. E. Wilson (eds.), Problems in Economic and Social Archaeology, pp. 375-399.

Mellars, P. A., 1976b. 'Fire, ecology, animal populations and man: a study of some ecological relationships in prehistory', Proceedings of the Prehistoric Society, 42:15-45.

Mellars, P. A., (ed.), 1978. The Early Post Glacial Settlement of Northern Europe. Duckworth, London.

Mellars, P. A. and Reinhardt, S., 1978. 'Patterns of Mesolithic land-use in Southern England: a geological perspective' in P. A. Mellars (ed.), 1978: 243-294.

Merton, R. K., 1957. Social Theory and Social Structure, Glencoe. III.

Mitchell, B., 1969. 'The potential output of meat as estimated from natural and park populations of red deer' in M. N. Bannerman and K. L. Blaxter (eds.), The Husbanding of Red Deer, pp. 16-28. The Highlands and Islands Development Board and the Rowett Research Institute.

Moore, P. D. and Bellamy, D. L., 1973. Peatlands, Paul Elek, London.

Mörnsjö, T., 1971. 'Peatland types and their regional distribution in southern Sweden', Geologiska Foreningens i Stockholm Förhandlinger 93:587-600.

Mueller, J. W., 1974. 'The use of sampling in archaeology survey', Memoirs of the Society for American Archaeology, No. 28.

Naroll, R., 1962. 'Floor area and settlement population, American Antiquity, 27(4):587-589.

Noe-Nygaard, N., 1974. 'Mesolithic hunting in Denmark illustrated by bone injuries caused by human weapons', Journal of Archaeological Science 1:217-248.

Novakowski, N. S., 1967. 'The winter bioenergetics of a beaver population in northern latitudes', Canadian Journal of Zoology, 45(6):1107-1118.

Odum, E. P., 1971. Fundamentals of Ecology.Saunders, London (3rd edition).

Oloff, H. B. 1951. 'Zur Biologie und Okologie des Wildschweines', Beitrage zur Tierkunde und Tierzucht, 2. Frankfurt-am-Main.

Osborne, P. J., 1971. 'Insect faunas of late Devensian and Flandrian age from Church Stretton, Shropshire', Royal Society Phil. Trans. B. Vol. 263, pp. 327-367.

Oswalt, W. H., 1976. An Anthropological Analysis of Food-Getting Technology John Wiley, London.

Petersen, R. L., 1955. North American Moose, University of Toronto Press, Toronto.

Perrin, R. M. and Hodge, C. A. H., 1965. 'The soils of the Cambridge region' in J. A. Steers (ed.), The Cambridge Region, pp. 68-84, Cambridge.

Perrin, R. M., Willis, E. H. and Hodge, C. A. H., 1964. 'Dating of humus podsols by residual radiocarbon activity', Nature 202:165-6.

Phillips, C. W., 1951. 'The fenland research committee: its past achievements and future prospects' in W. F. Grimes (ed.), Aspects of Archaeology in Britain and Beyond, pp. 258-273. Edwards, London.

Phillips, C. W., (ed.), 1970. 'The fenland in Roman Times', Royal Geographical Society Research Series 5. London.

Phillipson, J., 1966. Ecological Energetics. Arnold, London.

Plog, F. T., 1974. The Study of Prehistoric Change, Academic Press, London.

Price, T. D., 1978. 'Mesolithic settlement systems in the Netherlands' in P. Mellars (ed.) The Early Post-glacial Settlement of Northern Europe, pp. 81-114. Duckworth, London.

Prior, R., 1968. The Roe Deer of Cranbourne Chase, Oxford University Press, London.

Rackham, O., 1976. Trees and Woodlands in the English Landscape, Dent, London.

Rankine, W. F., 1953. 'A study of quartzite maceheads: functional interpretation and perforation technique', Archaeological Newsletter, 4(12): 186-8.

Rankine, G. F. and Dimbleby, G. W., 1960. 'Further investigations at a Mesolithic site at Oakhanger, Selboune, Hants.', Proceedings of the Prehistoric Society, 26:246-62.

Renfrew, C. A., 1972. The Emergence of Civilisation: The Cyclades and the Aegean in the Third Millennium B.C. Methuen, London.

Rhoades, R. E., 1978. 'Archaeological use and abuse of ecological concepts and studies: the ecotone example', American Antiquity, 43(4):608-14.

Roe, F. G., 1970. The North American Buffalo: A Critical Study of the Species in its Wild State. Toronto Univ. Press, Toronto (2nd edition).

Rybnicek, K., 1973. 'A comparison of the present and past mire communities of Central Europe' in H. J. D. Birks and R. G. West (eds.) Quaternary Plant Ecology, pp. 237-62. Blackwell, Oxford.

Schiffer, M. B., 1976. Behavioural Archaeology, Academic Press, London.

Schiffer, M. B. and Rathje, W. L., 1973. 'The efficient exploitation of the archaeological record' in C. L. Redman (ed.) Research and Theory in Current Archaeology, pp. 169-180. Wiley Interscience, London.

Schloeth, R., 1961. 'Einige Verhaltensweisen im Hirschrudel', Revue Suisse de Zoologie, 68(2):241-247.

Sims, R. E., 1973. 'Anthropogenic factors in East Anglian vegetative history' in H. J. D. Birks and R. L. West (eds). Quaternary Plant Ecology, pp. 223-36. Blackwell, Oxford.

Sims, R. E., 1978. 'Man and vegetation in Norfolk' in S. Limbrey and J. G. Evans (eds.), The Effect of Man on the Landscape: The Lowland Zone, Council for British Archaeology Research Report 21., pp. 57-62. London.

Simmons, I. G., 1969. 'Evidence for vegetative changes associated with Mesolithic man in Britain' in P. J. Ucko and G. W. Dimbleby (eds.), The Domestication and Exploitation of Plants and Animals, pp. 113-119. Duckworth, London.

Simmons, I. G. and Dimbleby, G. W., 1974. 'The possible role of ivy in the Mesolithic of western Europe', Journal of Archaeological Science I(3):291-296.

Smith, A. G., 1970. 'The influence of Mesolithic and Neolithic man on British vegetation: a discussion' in R. G. West and D. Walker (eds.) Studies in the Vegetational History of the British Isles, pp. 81-96. Cambridge Univ. Press, Cambridge.

Soper, J. D., 1941. 'History, range and home life of the northern bison', Ecological Monographs II:347-412.

Sparks, B. W. and West, R. G., 1965. 'The relief and drift deposits' in J. A. Steers (ed.) The Cambridge Region, pp. 18-40. Cambridge.

Steward, J., 1955. Theory of Culture Change. University of Illinois Press, Urbana.

Streuver, S., 1968. 'Woodland subsistence-settlement systems in the lower Illinois valley' in L. R. Binford and S. R. Binford (eds.), New Perspectives in Archaeology, pp. 285-312. Aldine, Chicago.

Streuver, S., 1971. 'Comments on archaeological data requirements and research strategy', American Antiquity, 36(1):9-19.

Sturdy, D. A., 1975. 'Some reindeer economies in prehistoric Europe', in E. S. Higgs (ed.) Palaeoeconomy, pp. 55-96. Cambridge University Press, Cambridge.

Sturge, W. A., 1912. 'Implements of the later Palaeolithic 'cave' periods in East Anglia', Proceedings of the Prehistoric Society of East Anglia, Vol. 1, Part II, pp. 210-232.

Taber, R. D., 1963. 'Land use and native cervid populations in America north of Mexico', Transactions of the International Union of Game Biologists 6:201-225.

Tansley, A. G., 1965. The British Isles and their Vegetation, Cambridge University Press, Cambridge (4th edition).

Taylor, C. C., 1973. The Cambridgeshire Landscape, London.

Tegner, H. S., 1951. The Roe Deer, Their History, Habitats and Pursuit, Batchworth Press, London.

Thomas, D. H., 1972. 'A computer simulation model of great basin Shoshonean Settlement patterns' in D. L. Clarke (ed.) Models in Archaeology, pp. 671-704. Methuen, London.

Tilley, C. Y., 1979. 'Conceptual frameworks for the explanation of socio-cultural change' in N. Hammond, G. Isaac and I. Hodder (eds.) The Pattern of the Past: Studies in Honour of David L. Clarke, Cambridge Univ. Press. (in press).

Tood, K. V. U., 1947. A Mesolithic Settlement on Lackford Heath, Unpublished manuscript, British Museum.

Vita Finzi, C. and Higgs, E. S., 1970. 'Prehistoric economies in the Mount Carmel area of Palestine: site catchment analysis', Proceedings of the Prehistoric Society, 36:1-37.

Walker, D., 1970. 'Direction and rate in some British post-glacial hydroseres' in D. Walker and R. G. West (eds.) Studies in the Vegetational History of the British Isles, pp. 117-140. Cambridge Univ. Press, Cambridge.

Walters, S. M., 1967. List of the Vascular Plants of Wicken Fen, National Trust Guide No. 3, Ipswich.

Watt, A. S., 1938. 'The climate of Cambridgeshire' in H. C. Darby (ed.) The Cambridge Region, pp. 31-43. Cambridge.

Webb, W. L., 1960. 'Forest wildlife management in Germany', Journal of Wildlife Management, 23:147-161.

Weissner, P., 1974. 'A functional estimation of population from floor area', American Antiquity, 39 (2):343-350.

Westlake, D. F., 1963. 'Comparisons of plant productivity', Biological Reviews of the Cambridge

White, J. M., 1932. 'The fens of North Armagh', <u>Proceedings of the Royal Irish Academy</u>, Vol. 40:233-83.

White, J. P. and Thomas, D. H., 1972. 'What mean these stones? Ethno-taxonomic models and archaeological interpretations in the New Guinea highlands' in D. L. Clarke (ed.) <u>Models in Archaeology</u>, pp. 275-308, Methuen, London.

Whittaker, R. H., 1970. <u>Communities and Evosystems</u>, Macmillan, London.

Williams, L., Thomas, D. H. and Bettinger, R., 1973. 'Notions to numbers: great basin settlements as polythethic sets' in C. L. Redman (ed.) <u>Research and Theory in Current Archaeology</u>, pp. 215-38. Wiley-Interscience, London.

Wilsson, L., 1971. 'Observations and experiments on the ethology of the European beaver (Castor fiber L.): a study in the development of phylo-genetically adapted behaviour in a highly specialized mammal', <u>Viltrevy</u> 8(3):117-260.

Wobst, H. M., 1974. 'Boundary conditions for Palaeolithic social systems: a simulation approach', <u>American Antiquity</u>, 39(2):147-78.

Woodburn, J., 1968. 'An introduction to Hadza ecology' in R. B. Lee and I. De Vore (eds.) <u>Man the Hunter</u>, pp. 49-55. Aldine, Chicago.

Worssam, B. C. and Taylor, J. H., 1969. <u>Geology of the Country Around Cambridge</u>, Memoirs of the Geological Survey, H.M.S.O. London.

Wymer, J. J., 1962. 'Excavations at the Maglemosian sites at Thatcham, Berkshire, England', <u>Proceedings of the Prehistoric Society</u>, 28:329-61.

Wymer, J. J., 1977 (ed.). <u>Gazetteer of Mesolithic sites in England and Wales</u>, Council for British Archaeology, London.

Zubrow, E. B. W., 1971. 'Carrying capacity and dynamic equilibrium in the prehistoric south-west', <u>American Antiquity</u>, 36(4):127-38.

Zubrow, E. B. W., 1975. Prehistoric Carrying Capacity: A Model. Cummings, Menlo Park, California.

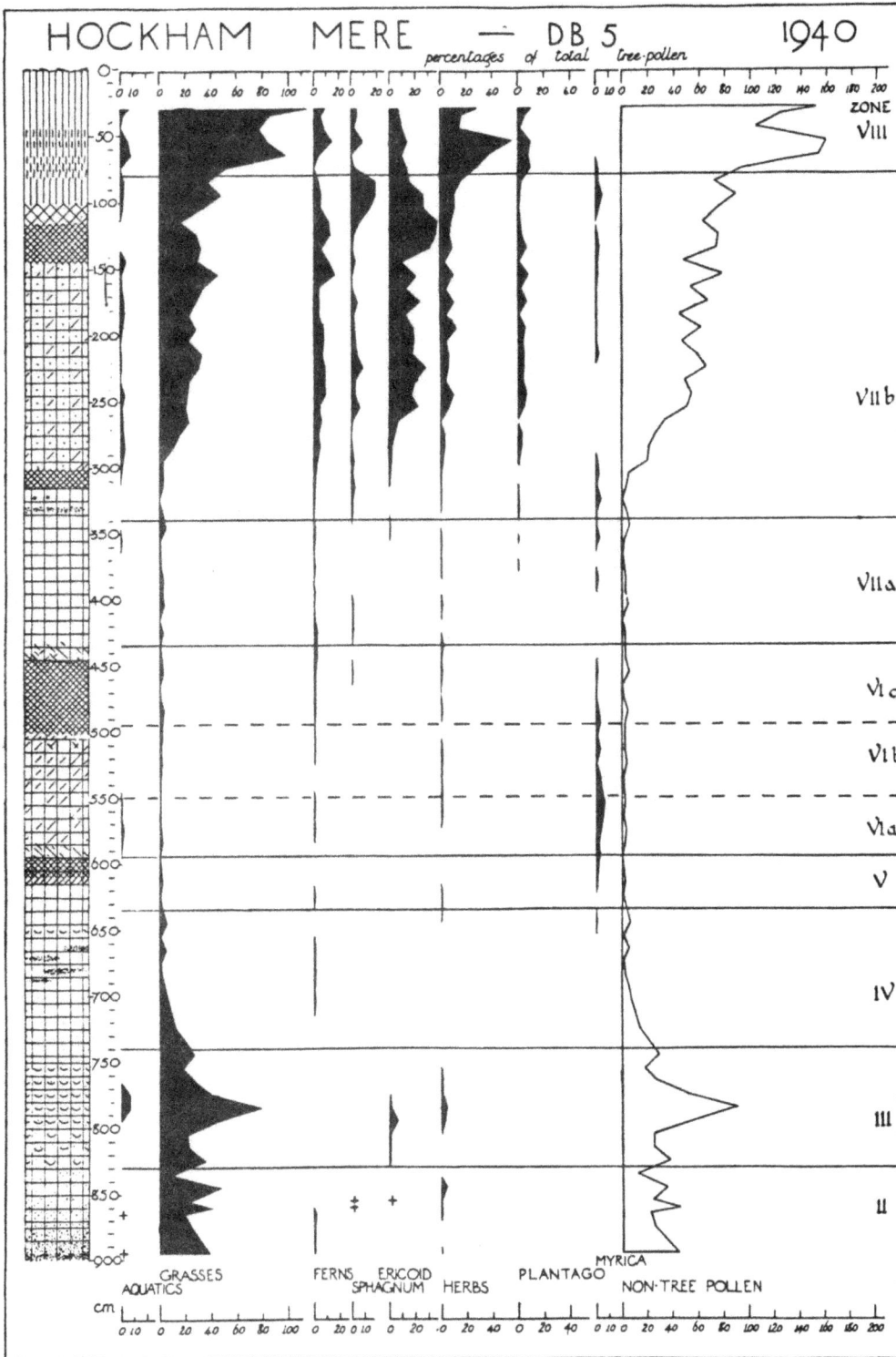

Fig. 1   Non-tree pollen diagram for DB5, Hockham Mere.   This is an
          uninterrupted series from deep water (Source: Godwin and
          Tallantire, 1951).

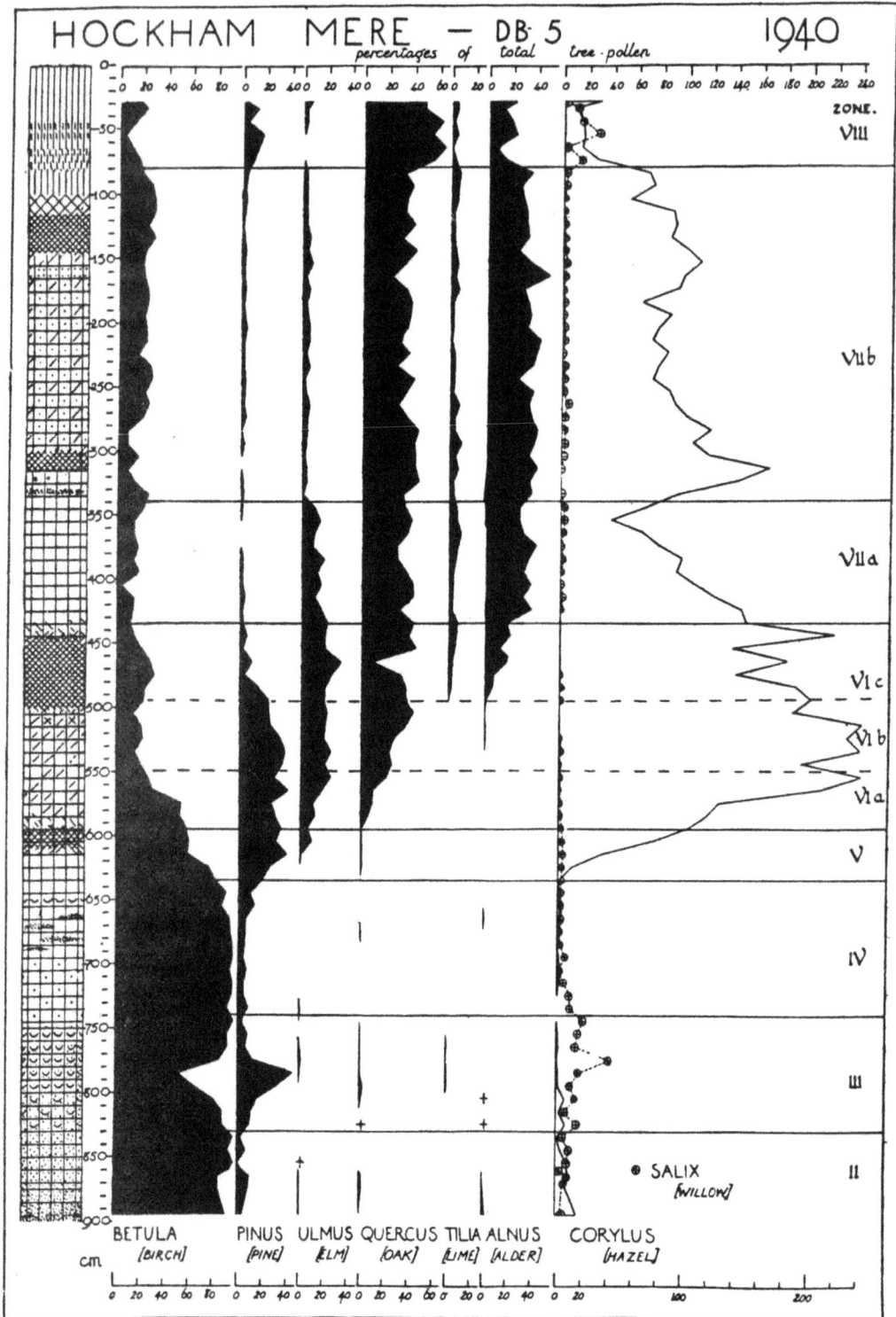

HOCKHAM MERE — DB·5   1940
percentages of total tree·pollen

Fig. 2   Tree pollen diagram for DB5, Hockham Mere (Source: Godwin and Tallantire, 1951).

66

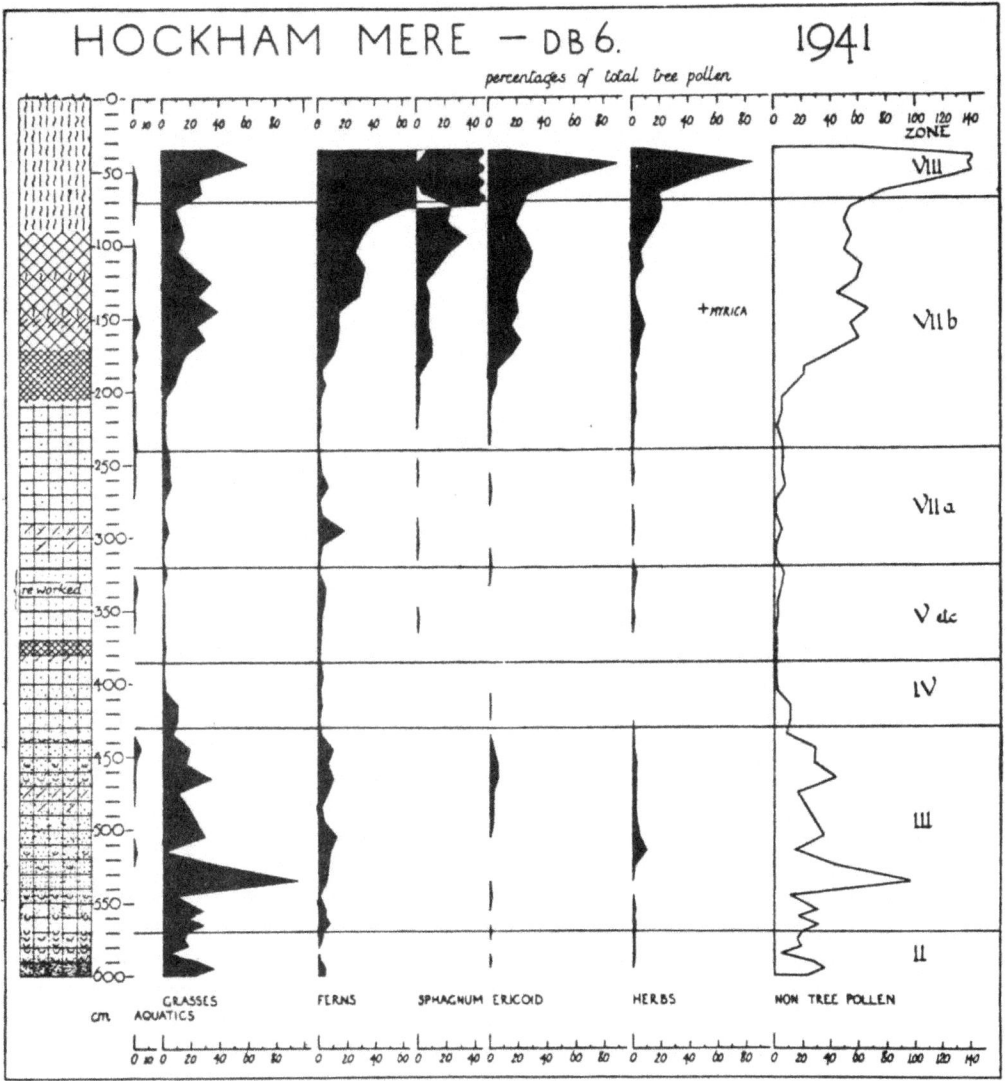

Fig. 3   Non-tree pollen diagram for DB6, Hockham Mere. The series is
           interrupted by the Late-boreal phase of low lake levels (Source:
           Godwin and Tallantire, 1951).

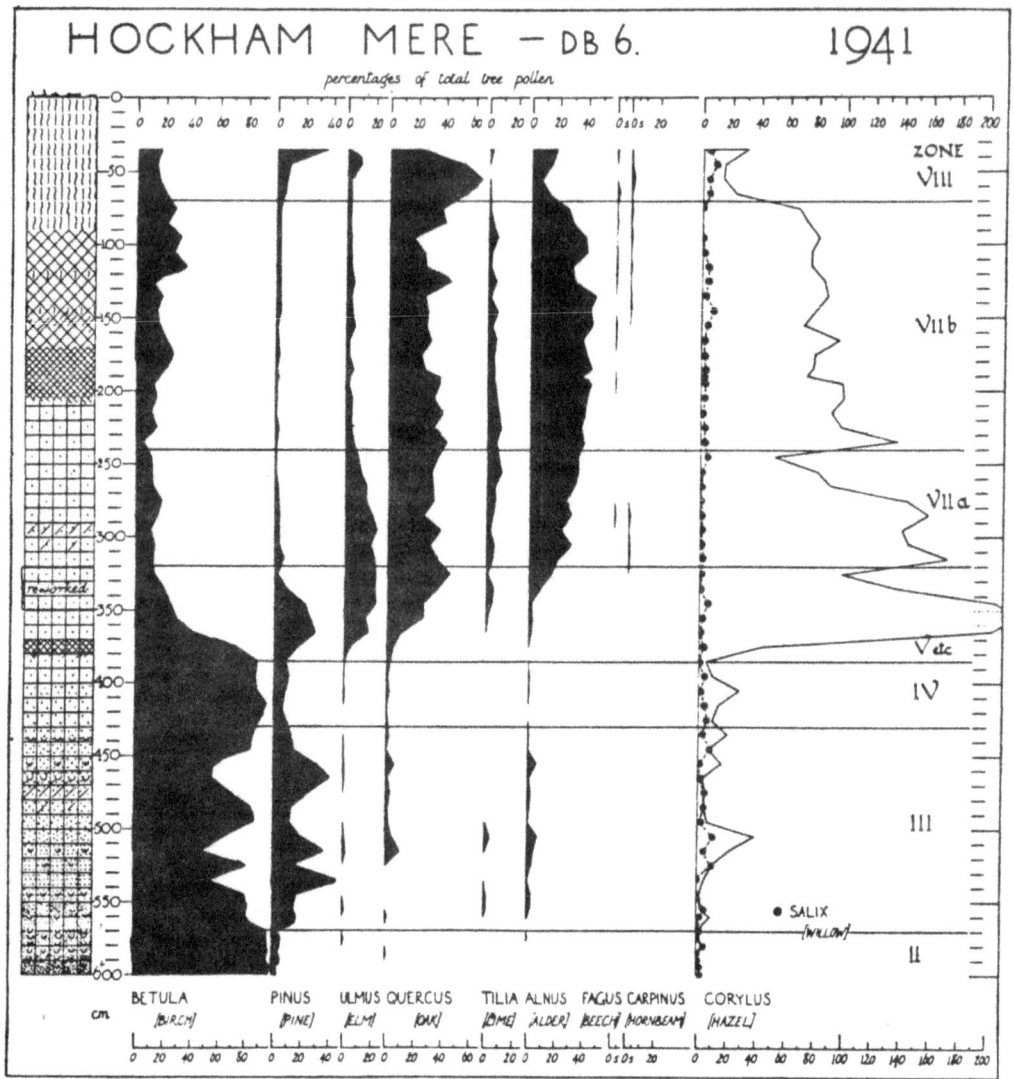

HOCKHAM MERE — DB 6.   1941

percentages of total tree pollen

ZONE

VIII

VIIb

VIIa

V dc

IV

III

II

● SALIX
[WILLOW]

cm

BETULA [BIRCH]   PINUS [PINE]   ULMUS [ELM]   QUERCUS [OAK]   TILIA [LIME]   ALNUS [ALDER]   FAGUS [BEECH]   CARPINUS [HORNBEAM]   CORYLUS [HAZEL]

Fig. 4   Tree pollen diagram for DB6, Hockham Mere (Source: Godwin and Tallantire, 1951).

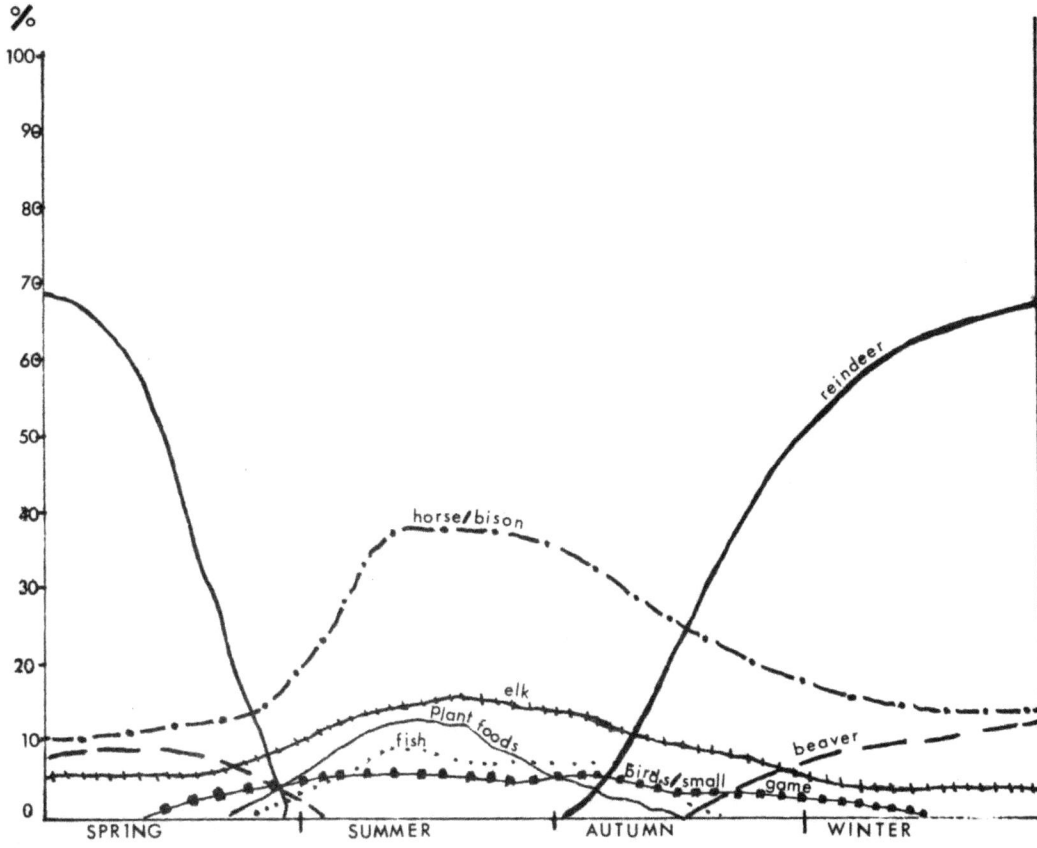

Fig. 5   Predicted resource use schedule for Late-glacial communities in the Cambridge region.

tool numbers

0   10   20   30   40   50   60   70   80

scrapers

scrapers/burins

burins & spalls

burin/truncated blade

truncated blades

retouched blades

backed blades

penknife point

micro-burin

cores

tools - 103
waste - 529

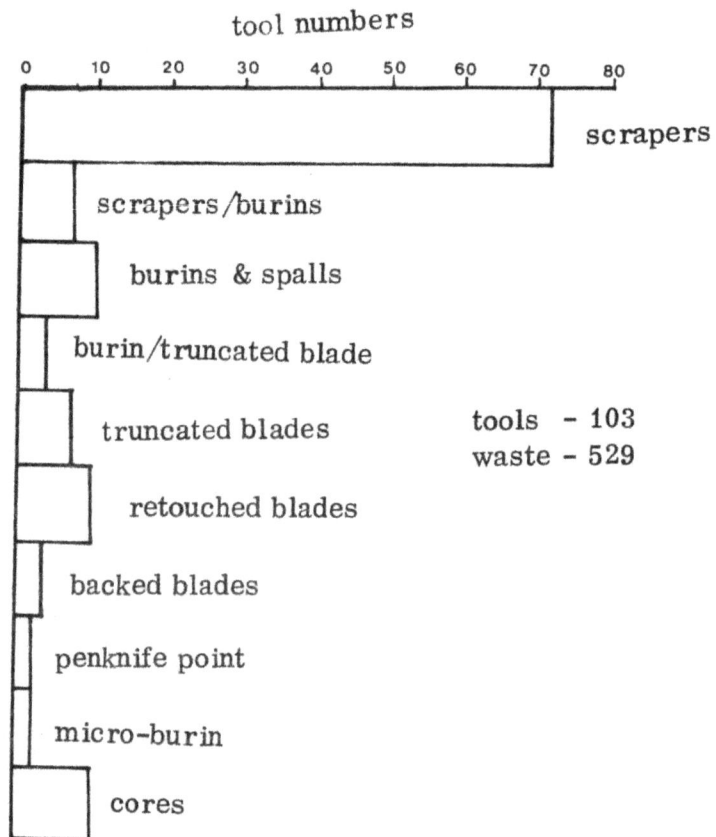

Fig. 6   Proportional representation of tool classes for the Late-glacial
site of Whiteway Drove, Swaffham Prior (Source: Jacobi, 1976).

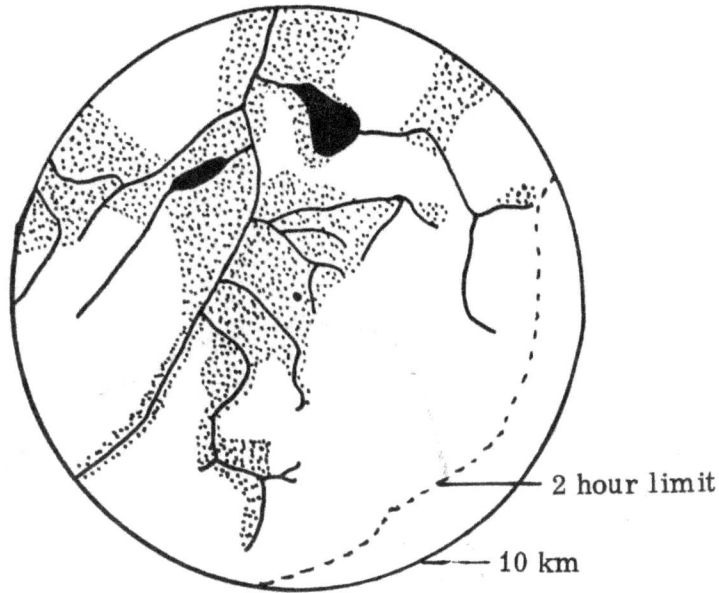

Fig. 7   Whiteway Drove, Swaffham Prior—site catchment analysis.

(Key: Fig. 33)

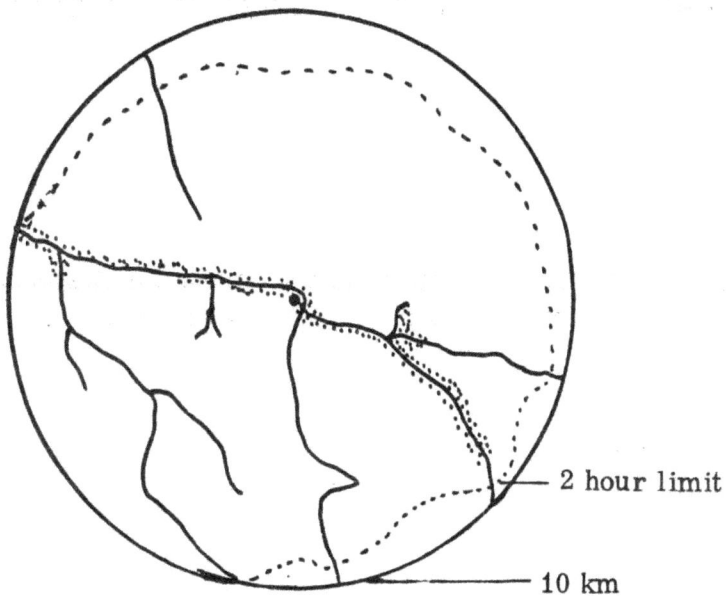

Fig. 8   London Bottom, Icklingham—site catchment analysis.

(Key: Fig. 33)

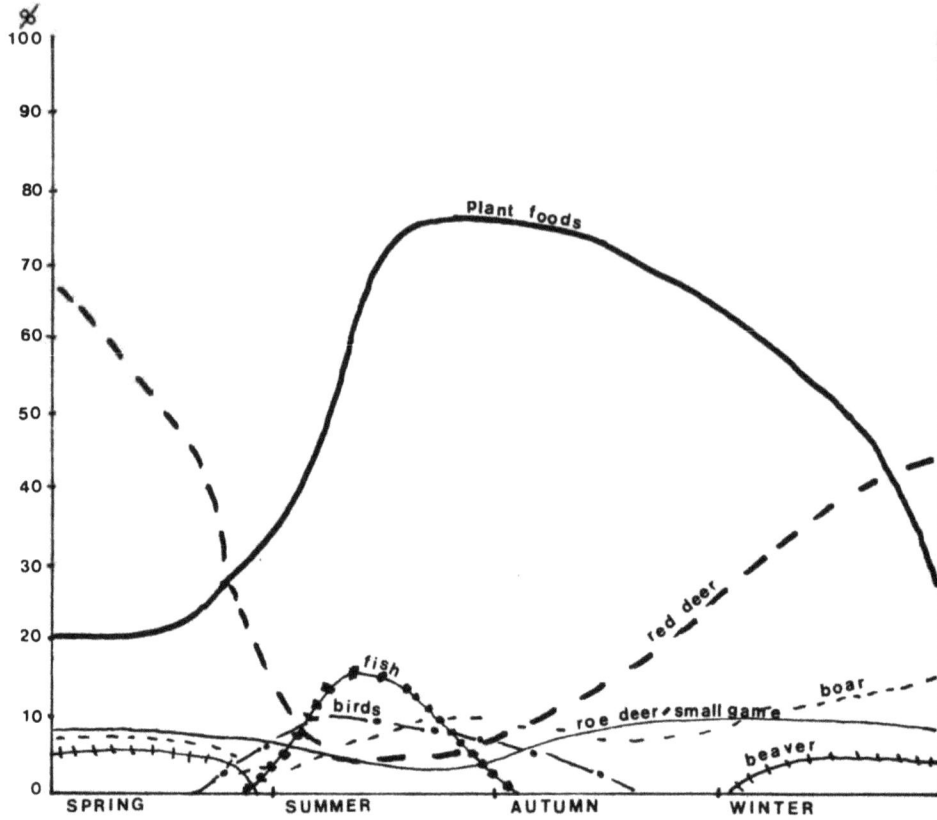

Fig. 9   Predicted resource use schedule for Atlantic Mesolithic
communities in the Cambridge region.

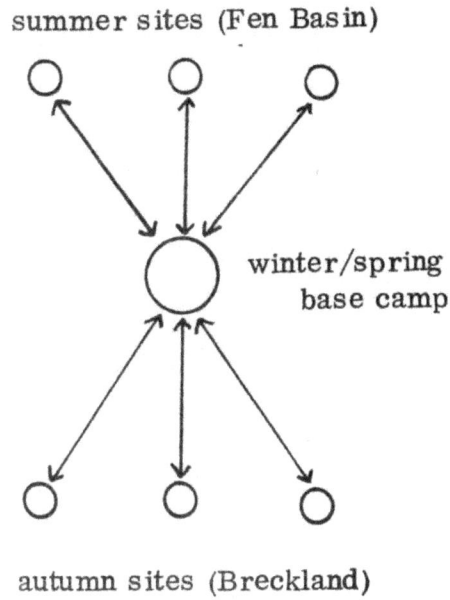

summer sites (Fen Basin)

winter/spring
base camp

autumn sites (Breckland)

Fig. 10   Model 1—settlement location.

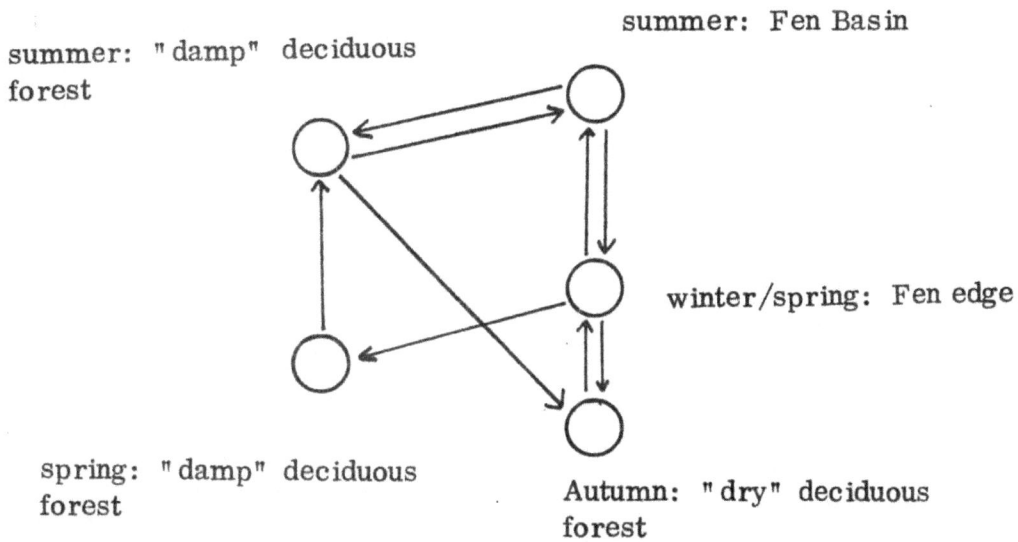

summer: Fen Basin

summer: "damp" deciduous
forest

winter/spring: Fen edge

spring: "damp" deciduous
forest

Autumn: "dry" deciduous
forest

Fig. 11   Model 2—settlement location.

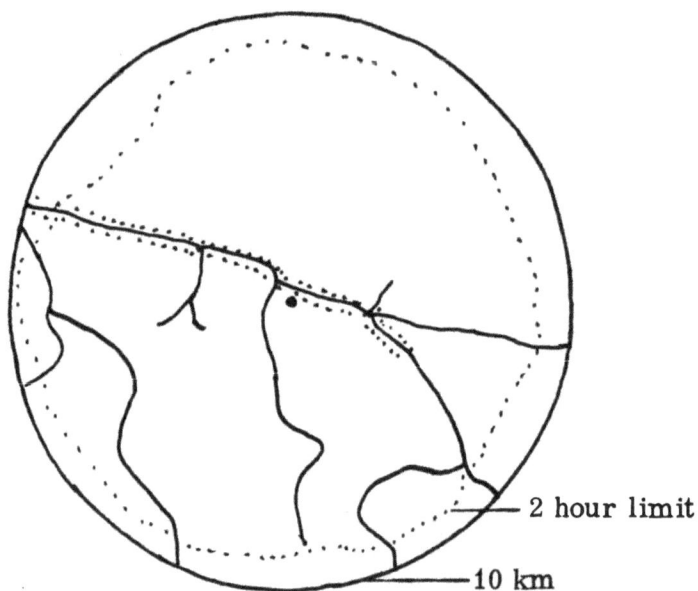

Fig. 12 Home Heath, Lackford—site catchment analysis.
(Key: Fig. 33)

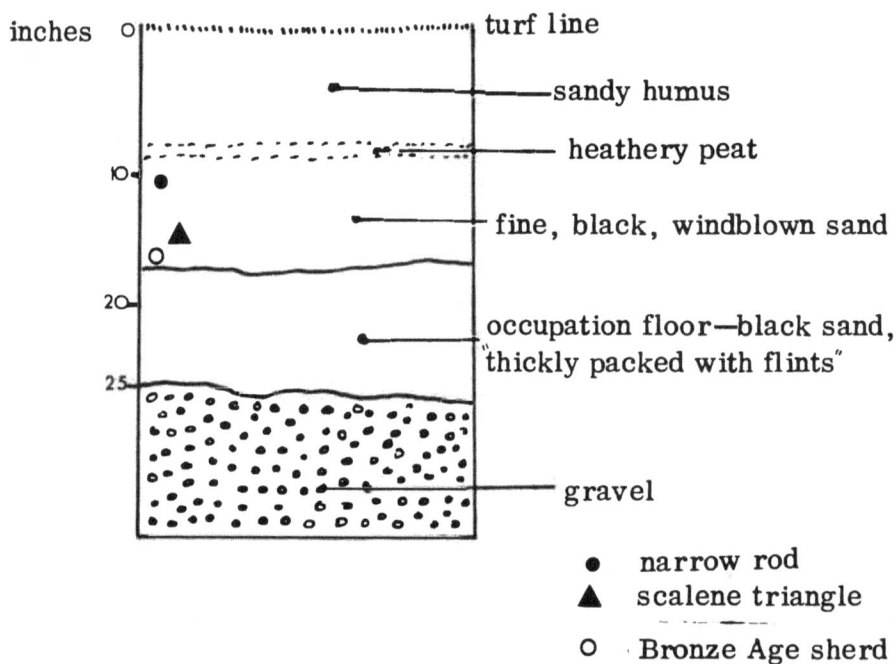

Fig. 13 Section through the Lackford structure (Source: Todd, 1947).

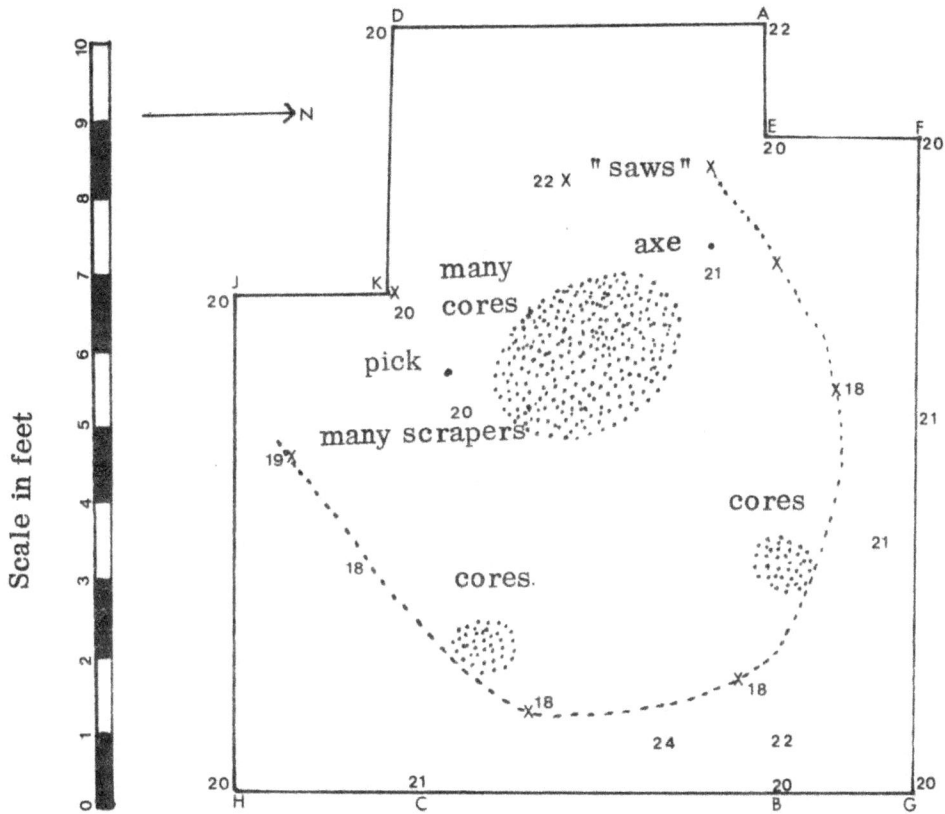

Fig. 14   Plan of the excavation at Lackford (Source: Todd, 1947).

Stippled areas indicate hearths.
Dashed area indicates the 'presumed outline of the hut"
Letter X indicates measured outline of the hut
Numbered figures indicate depth of floor base in inches

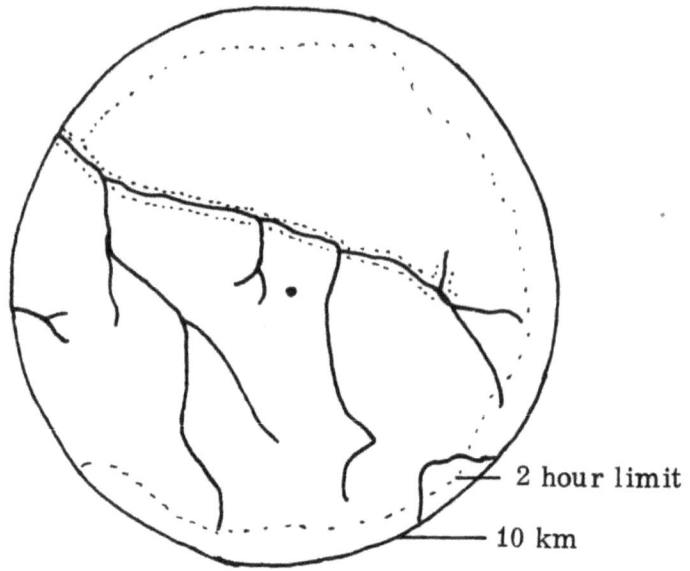

Fig. 15   Cavenham Heath—site catchment analysis.

(Key: Fig. 33)

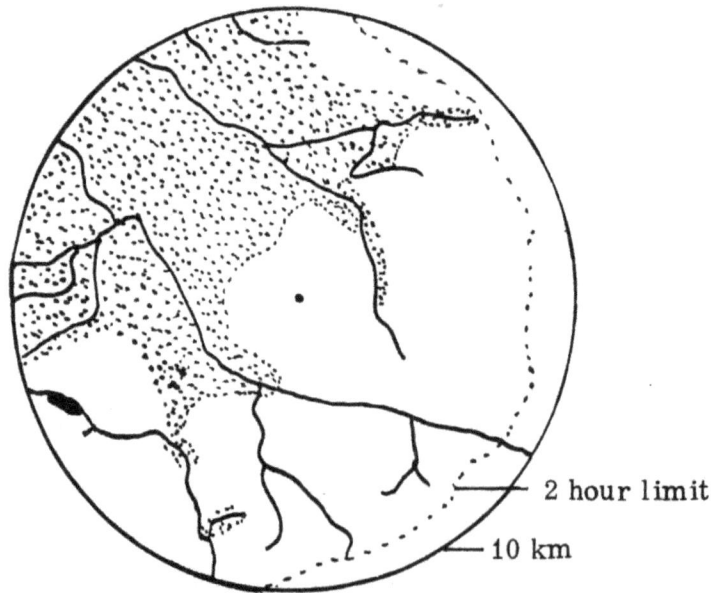

Fig. 16   Kenny Hill—site catchment analysis.

(Key: Fig. 33)

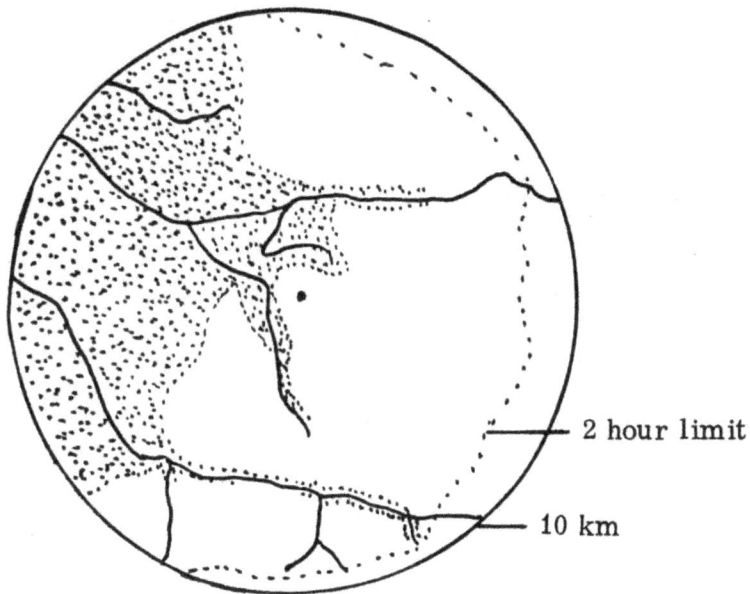

Fig. 17   Lakenheath—site catchment analysis.

(Key: Fig. 33)

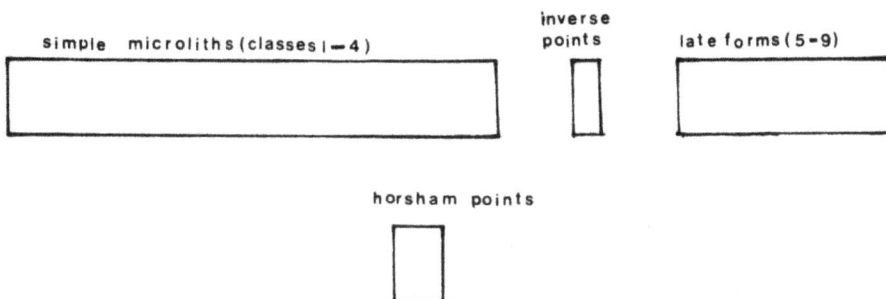

Fig. 18   Proportional representation of microlith classes, patinated
series, Lakenheath (Source: Jacobi, 1976).

inches

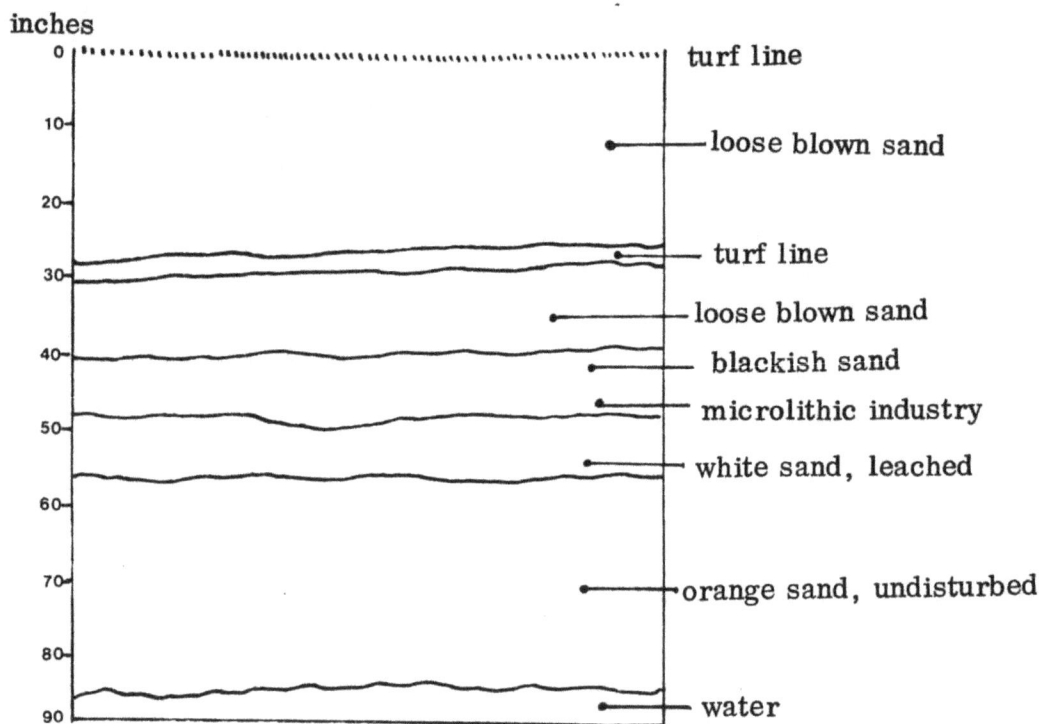

Fig. 19 Section through the general area of the Wangford industry (Source: Clark, 1932).

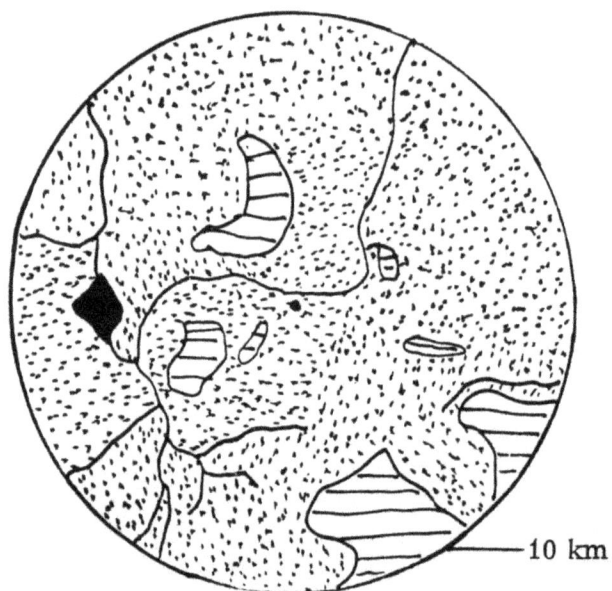

Fig. 20 Honey Hill—site catchment analysis.

(Key: Fig. 33)

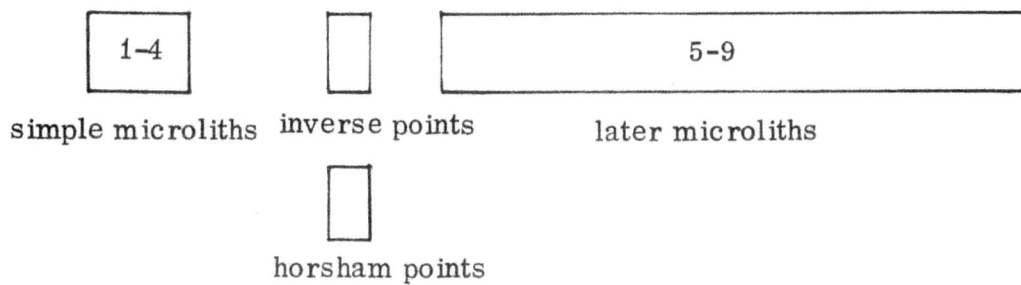

Fig. 21 Proportional representation of microlith classes, unpatinated
series, Lakenheath (Source: Jacobi, 1976).

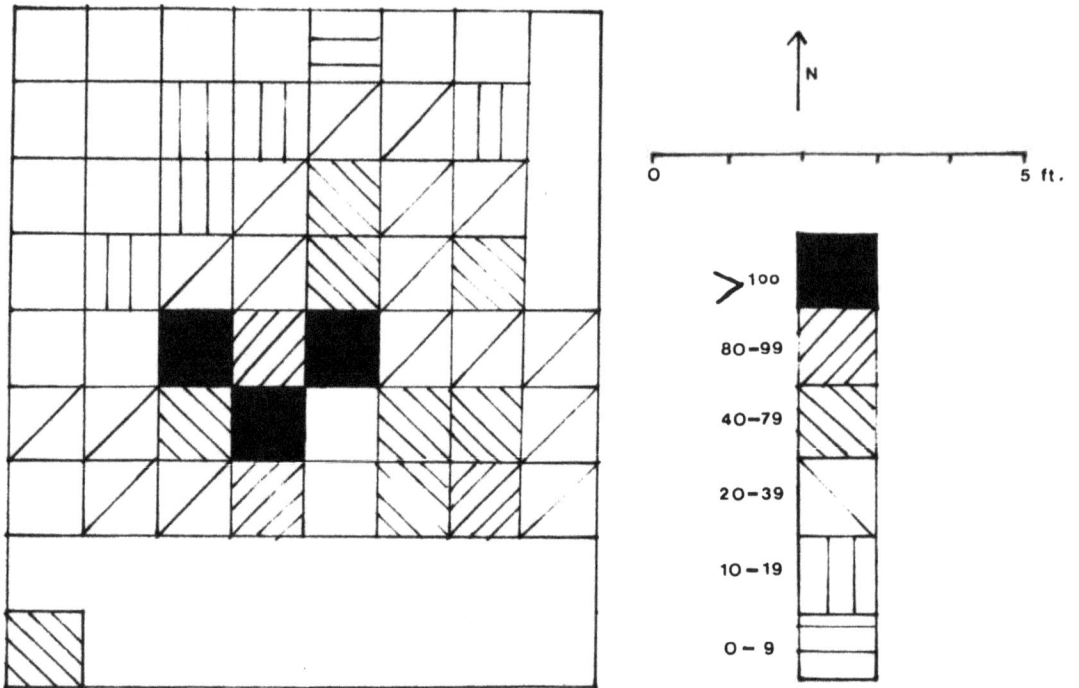

Fig. 22 Wangford, Oat Hill - spatial distribution of flint (Source: Jacobi, 1976)

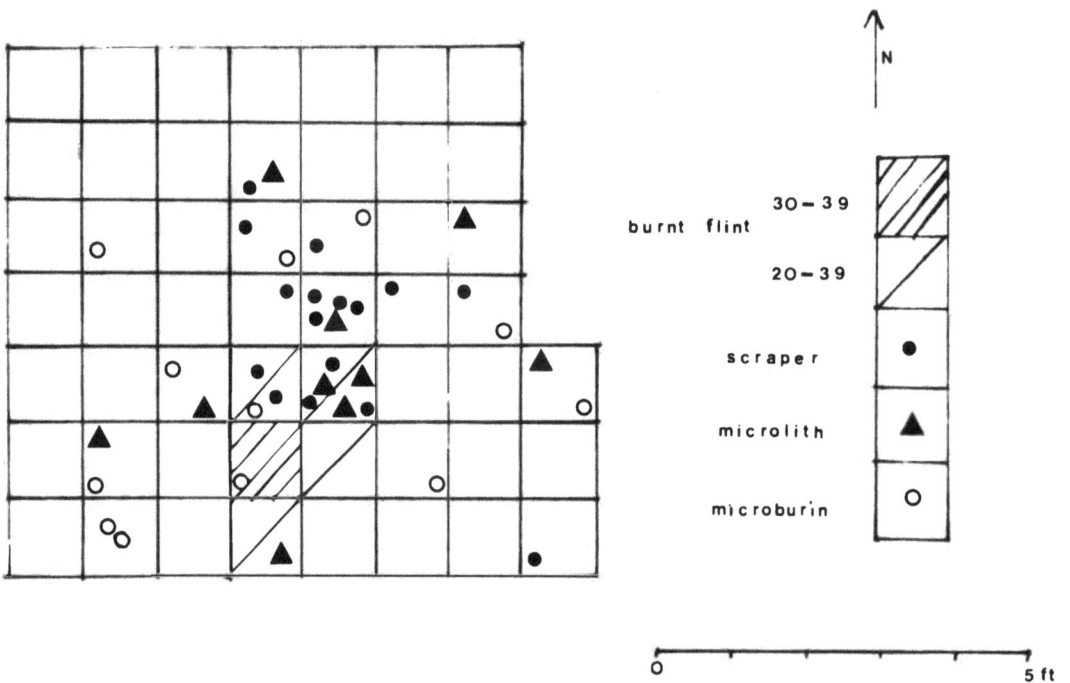

Fig. 23 Wangford, Oat Hill - spatial distribution of tool classes and burnt flint (Source: Jacobi, 1976)

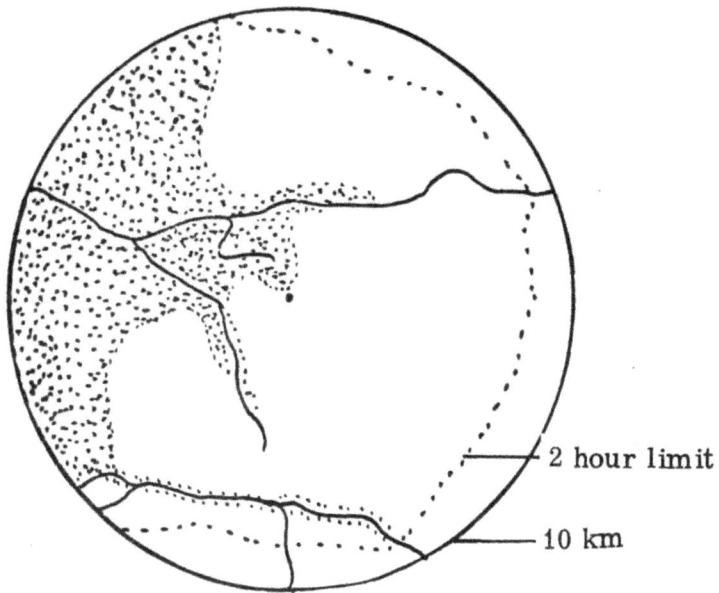

Fig. 24   Wangford, Oat Hill—site catchment analysis.
(Key: Fig. 33)

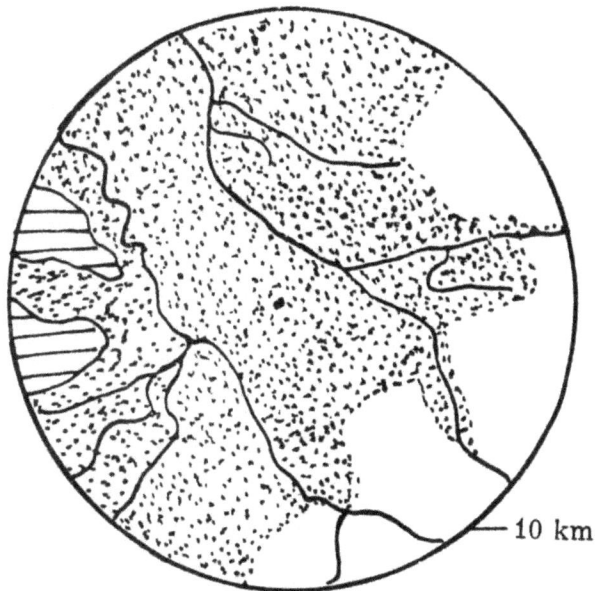

Fig. 25   Shippea Hill—site catchment analysis.

(Key: Fig. 33)

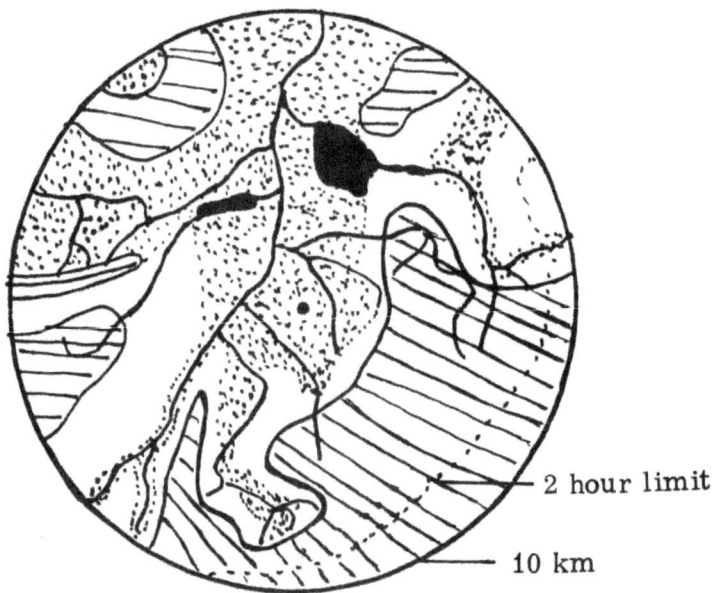

Fig. 26   Little Fen Drove—site catchment analysis.
(Key: Fig. 33)

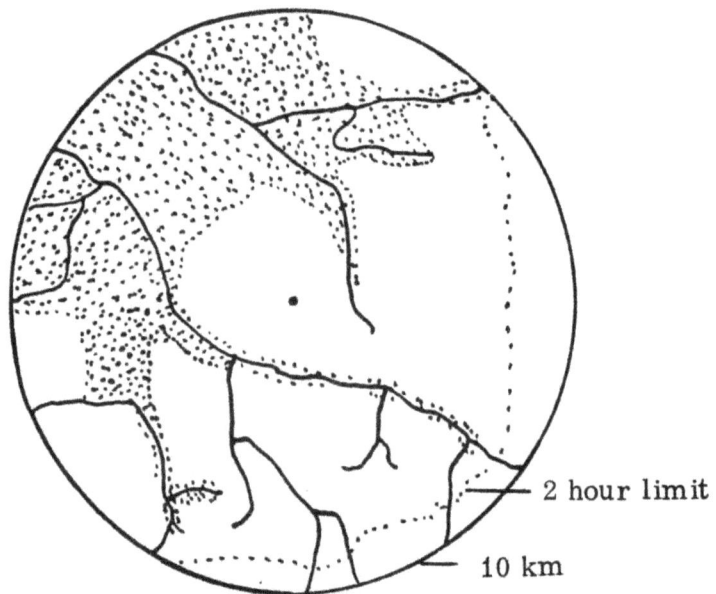

Fig. 27   Wilde Street, Beck Row—site catchment analysis.

(Key: Fig. 33)

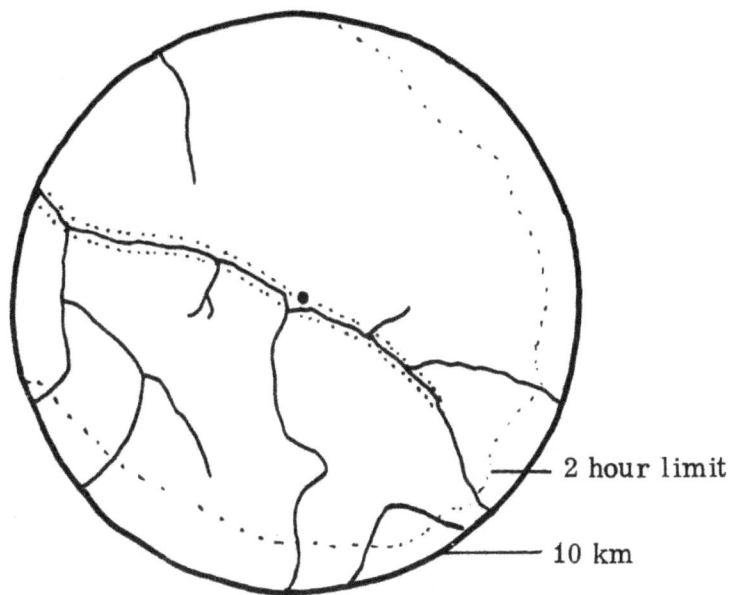

Fig. 28   Icklingham, London Bottom—site catchment analysis.

(Key: Fig. 33)

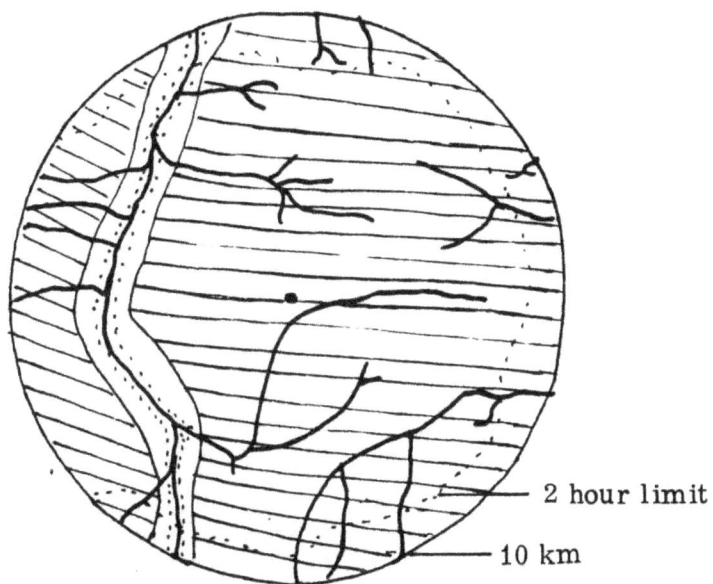

Fig. 29   Gamlingay—site catchment analysis.

(Key: Fig. 33)

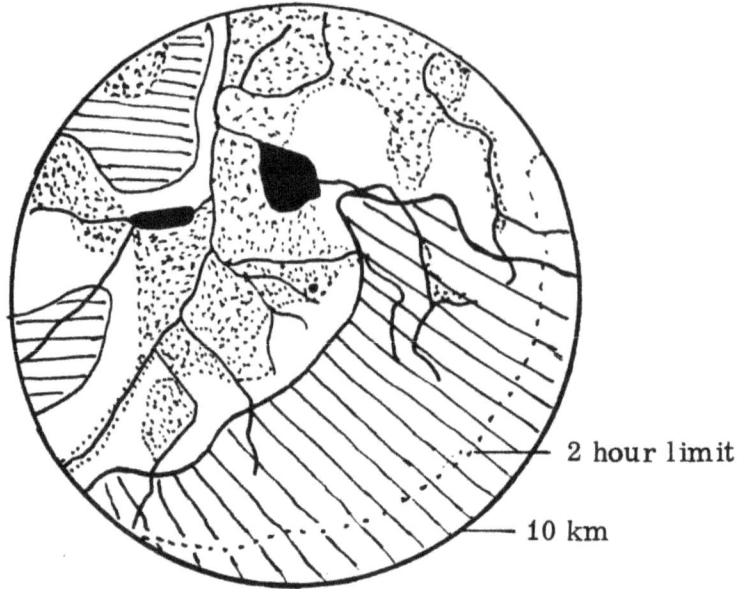

2 hour limit

10 km

Fig. 30   Hallard's Fen—site catchment analysis.

(Key: Fig. 33)

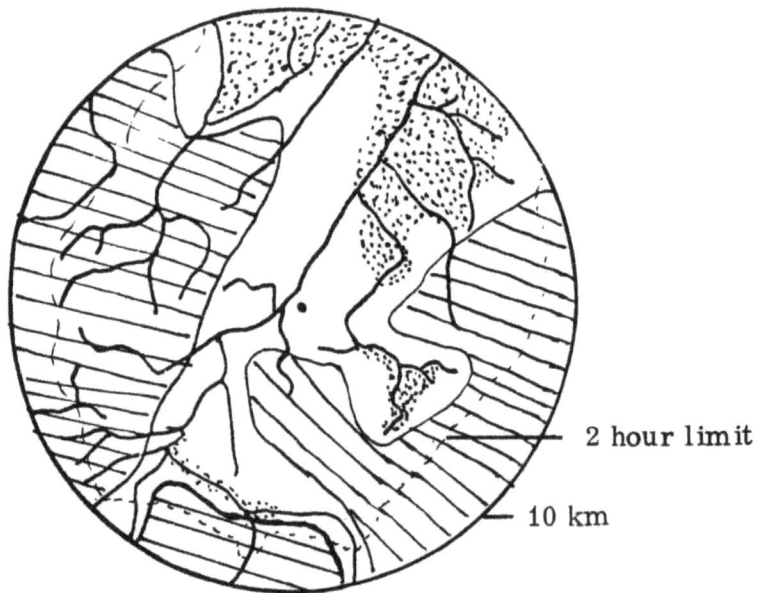

2 hour limit

10 km

Fig. 31   Fen Ditton—site catchment analysis.

(Key: Fig. 33)

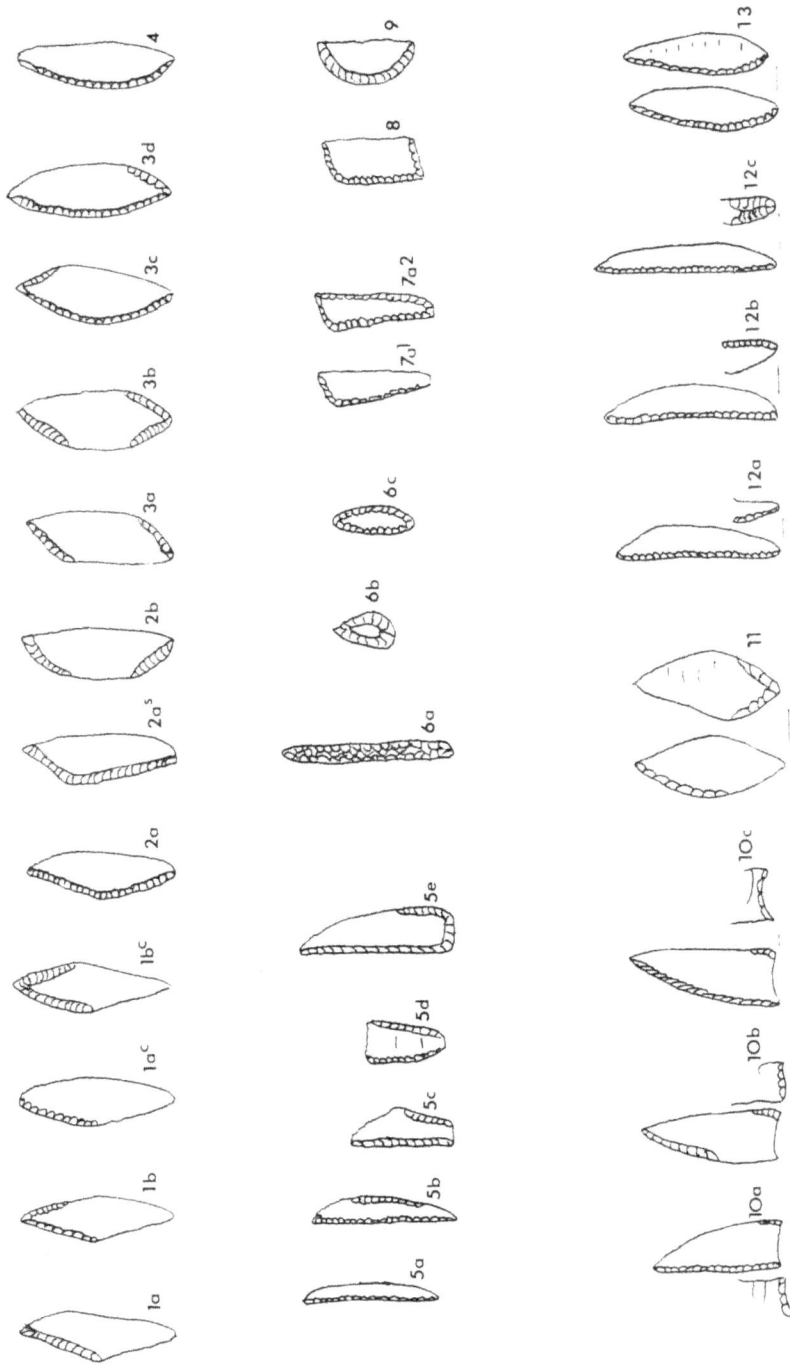

Fig. 32   Microlith classification. 1–4: broad blade forms. 5–9: narrow blade forms. 10: hollow based points.
11–13: inversely retouched points (Source: Jacobi 1976).

areas of the fen basin with a developing
oligotrophic lake ecology

tundra/light birch dominated woodland

Late-glacial sites

presumed fen areas

'dry' deciduous forest

'damp' deciduous forest

Mesolithic sites

Fig. 33   Key to site catchment studies

Plate 1   Aerial view along the Lark river valley looking north-west
           (Cambridge University collection: copyright reserved).

Plate 2   Aerial view of Wicken Fen (Cambridge University collection:
copyright reserved).

Plate 3   View from the Mildenhall area looking north-east across the
            fen-edge ecotone (Cambridge University collection: copyright
            reserved).

Plate 4   Vegetation patterning developing on the dry Breckland soils
(Cambridge University collection: copyright reserved).

Plate 5   Fenland microtopography and ancient river channels, Upwell
(Cambridge University collection: copyright reserved).

Table 1 The expected dietary importance of resources/annum in the Cambridge
region. The area where the resource is most likely to be abundant
and at which season exploitation is most likely is indicated. Only two
groups of plant foods are considered in the table. The total percentages for plant foods at the top of the table are those for all plant foods
consumed, including those considered in the table.

1 - 'damp' deciduous forest.
2 - 'dry' deciduous forest.
3 - 'damp' deciduous forest on the chalk escarpment.
4 - the fen basin.
5 - fen-edge ecotone.

Resource	Area	Season	Boreal	Atlantic
Plant foods	–	–	50	75
hazel	2, 5	autumn	10	25
rhizomes	4, 5	summer/autumn	10	15
aurochs	2, 3, 5	autumn/winter	8	2
elk	4, 5	autumn/winter	3	–
red deer	2, 5	autumn/winter/spring	17	8
roe deer	2, 5	autumn/winter/spring	7	3
boar	1, 4, 5	summer/winter	5	5
small game	–	–	2	1
beaver	4, 5	winter/spring	3	1
fish	4, 5	summer	3	3
wildfowl	4, 5	summer	2	2

Table 2   Proportional representation of microlith classes at the Lakenheath
           site (Source: Jacobi 1976)

microlith classes	% early site	% late site
1	48.4	7.65
2a	-	1.1
2b	3.3	-
3a	1.1	.53
3b	1.1	.26
3c	2.2	.26
3d	6.5	2.6
4	5.4	.79
5	4.4	10.3
5b	5.4	8.2
5c	-	-
5d	-	-
5e	2.2	1.06
6	-	1.32
7	15.1	51.2
8	-	3.4
9	2.2	2.64
horsham points		
A	-	-
B	2.04	-
C	2.2	.26
other points	2.2	2.37

Table 3   Observed (O.D.) and expected (E.D.) frequency distribution of
artifact classes and sites in the Cambridge region in relation to
soil zonation.

1:   Boulder clay soils—973 km^2
2:   Fen Basin soils—607 km^2
3:   Sandy Breckland soils—165 km^2
4:   Rendzinas/Terrace gravel loams—815 km^2

A: Mesolithic Tranchet axes
B: Mesolithic sites
C: Neolithic axes (flint and groundstone)
D: Neolithic groundstone axes
E: Neolithic sites (excluding M.II survey sites)
F: Neolithic projectile points (excluding Hurst & Driest Fen)

Soil Zone		1	2	3	4	total
A	O.D.	7	114	39	9	169
	E.D.	64.23	40.07	10.89	53.80	169
B	O.D.	1	7	15	1	24
	E.D.	9.12	5.69	1.54	7.64	24
C	O.D.	16	153	36	60	265
	E.D.	93.11	58.09	15.79	78.00	265
D	O.D.	6	58	27	52	143
	E.D.	54.35	33.96	9.21	45.31	143
E	O.D.	6	11	9	55	81
	E.D.	30.78	19.20	5.22	25.78	81
F	O.D.	2	33	96	22	153
	E.D.	58.15	36.27	9.86	48.71	153

Table 4   Observed (O.D.) and expected (E.D.) frequency distribution of artifact classes and sites in the Cambridge region in relation to ecological zonation.

1:    'Damp' deciduous forest on boulder clay and river terrace areas—1555 km^2

2:    'Dry' deciduous forest—116 km^2

3:    Fen vegetation—460 km^2

4:    'Damp' deciduous forest on chalk escarpment—135 km^2

5:    Fen edge ecotone—294 km^2

For artifact and site totals and explanation of artifact and site classification see Table 3.

Ecol. zone		1	2	3	4	5
A	O.D.	16	23	20	0	110
	E.D.	102.65	7.65	30.36	8.91	19.40
B	O.D.	1	0	4	0	19
	E.D.	14.57	1.08	4.31	1.26	2.75
C	O.D.	49	19	70	4	103
	E.D.	160.96	12.00	47.61	13.97	30.43
D	O.D.	31	3	11	10	88
	E.D.	86.86	6.47	25.69	7.54	16.42
E	O.D.	54	6	5	0	16
	E.D.	49.20	3.67	14.55	4.27	9.30
F	O.D.	13	41	13	3	83
	E.D.	92.93	6.93	27.44	8.06	17.57

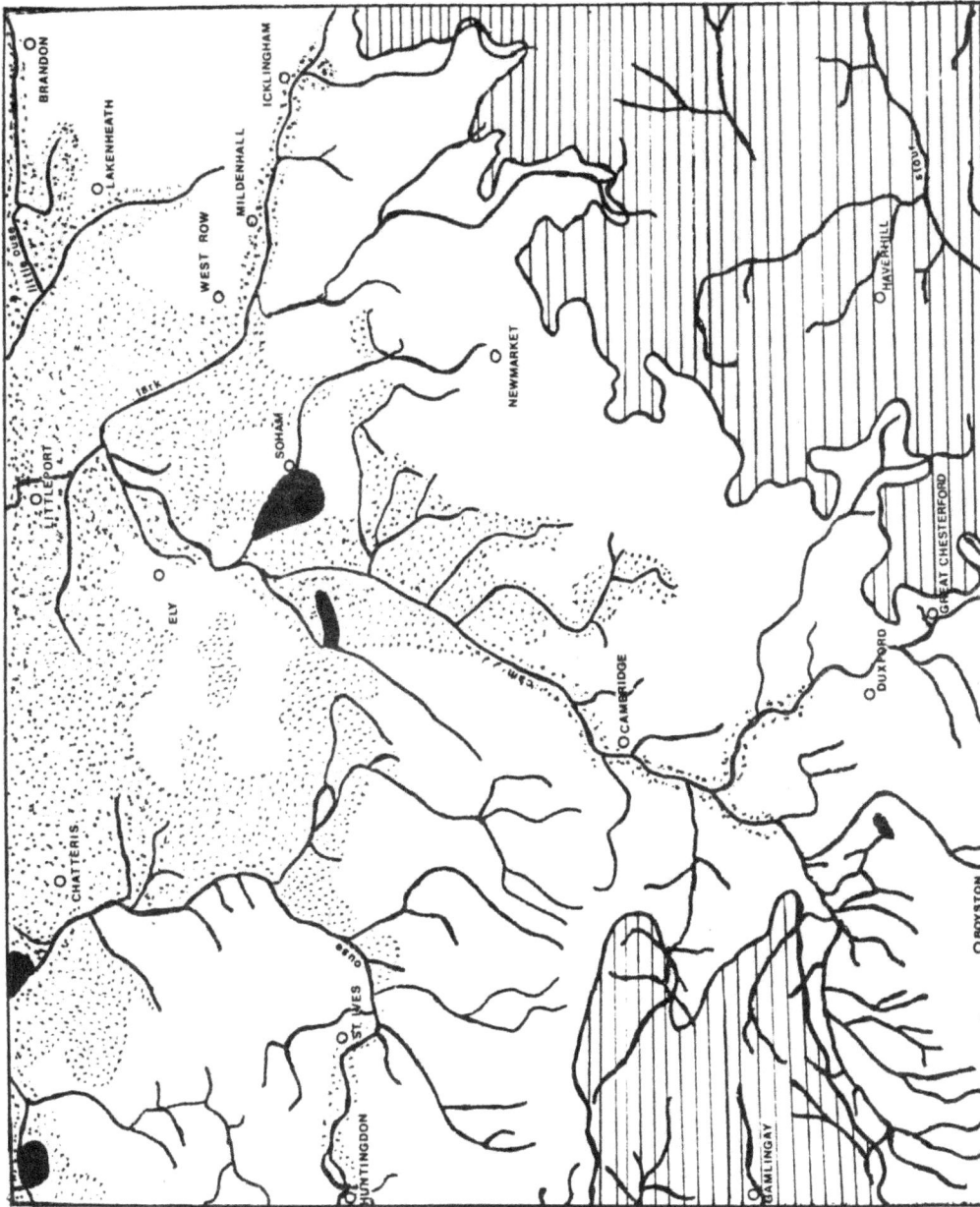

Map A: The Cambridge region;   general topographical features and modern settlement.

LAND OVER
200 FT

FENLAND

0   3   6 km

N

A

BRANDON
LAKENHEATH
WEST ROW
MILDENHALL
ICKLINGHAM
NEWMARKET
SOHAM
LITTLEPORT
ELY
CAMBRIDGE
DUXFORD
GREAT CHESTERFORD
HAVERHILL
STOUR
ROYSTON
GAMLINGAY
HUNTINGDON
ST IVES
CHATTERIS
OUSE
IVEL
LARK
CAM

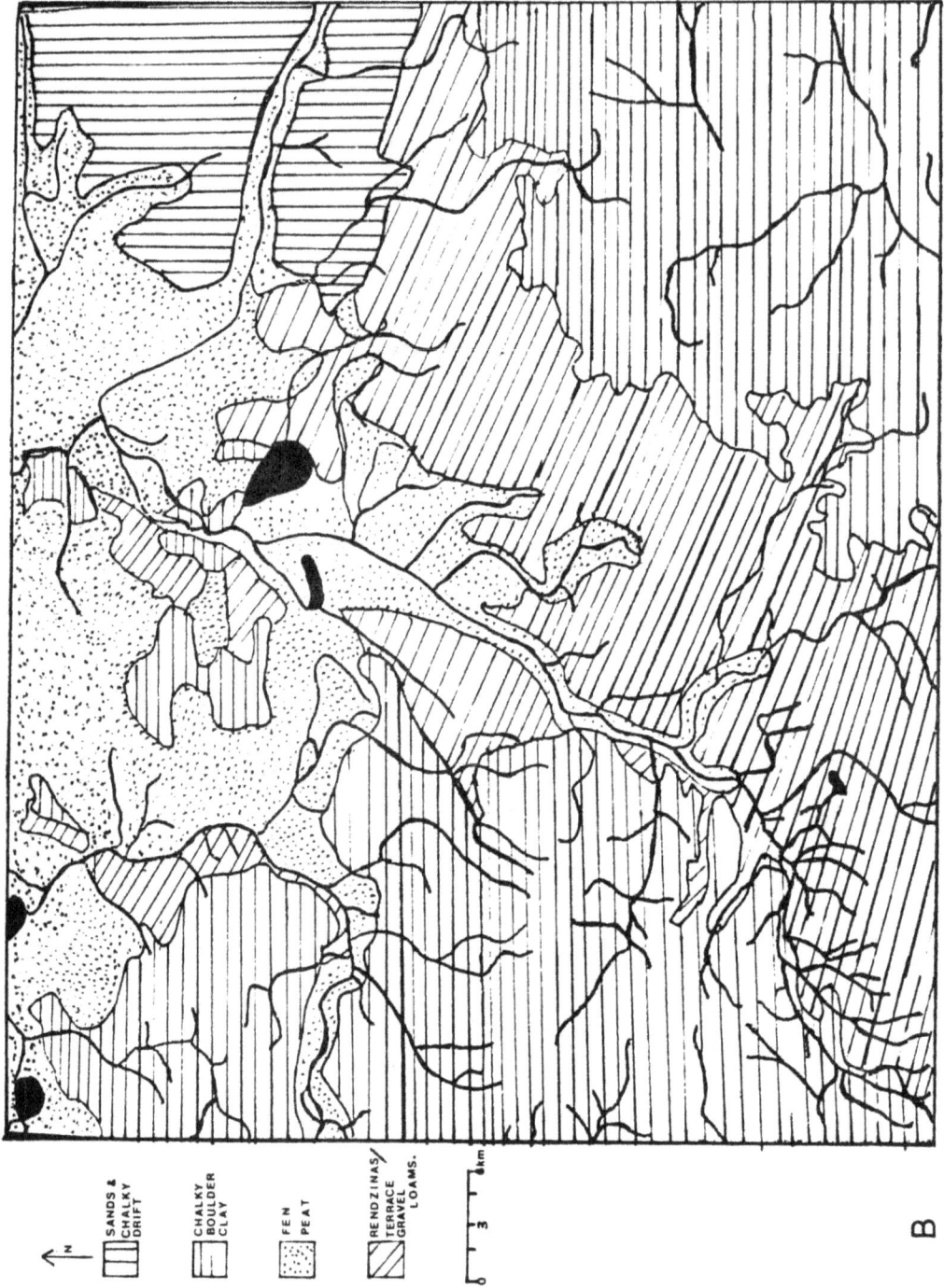

Map B: The generalized distribution of soils within the Cambridge region.

SANDS &
CHALKY
DRIFT

CHALKY
BOULDER
CLAY

FEN
PEAT

RENDZINAS/
TERRACE
GRAVEL
LOAMS.

0   3   6km

B

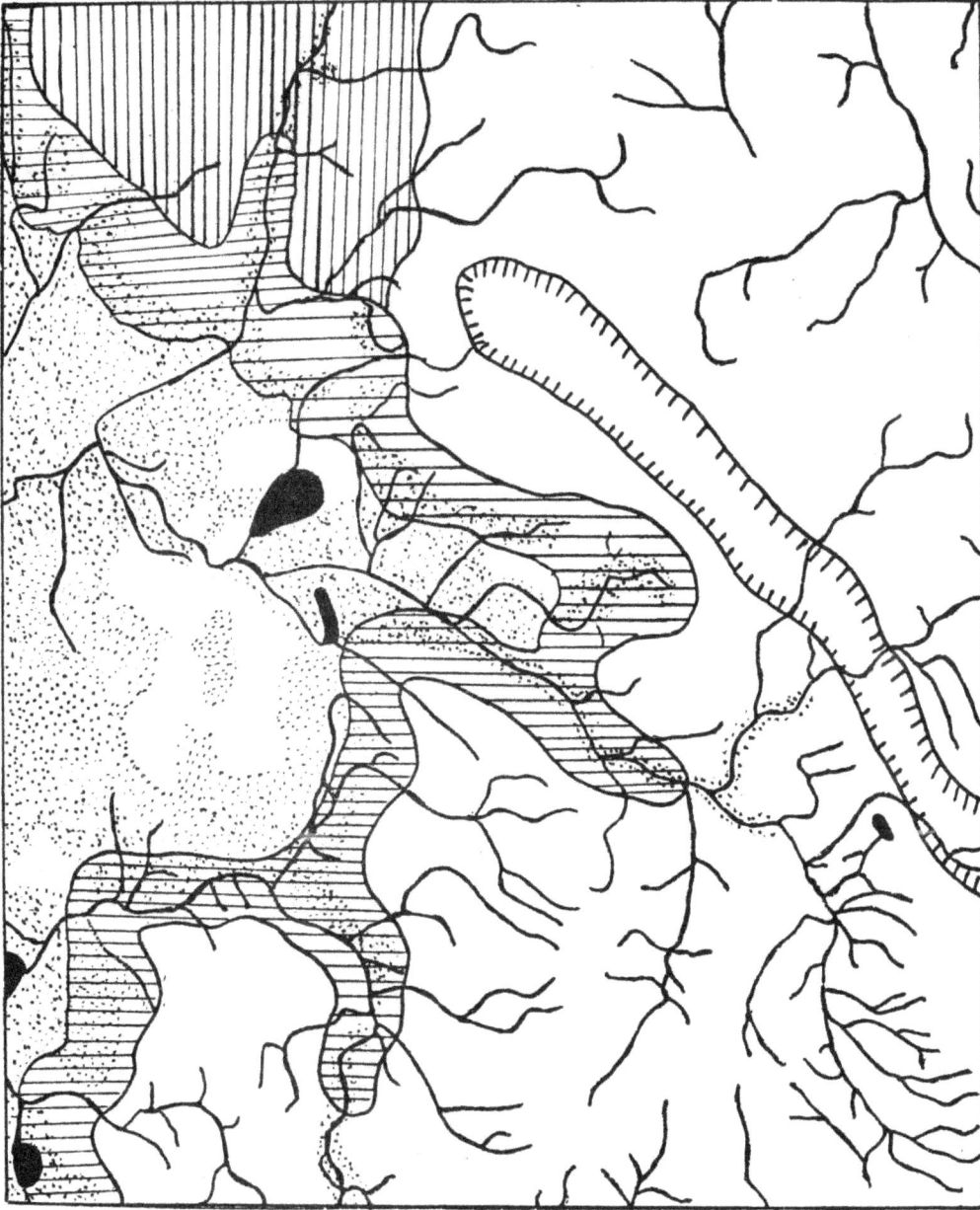

Map C: The major ecological zones of the Cambridge region.

Legend:

- FEN—EDGE ECOTONE
- "DRY" DECID. FOREST
- FEN VEGETATION
- "DAMP" DECID. FOREST ON CHALK ESCARPMENT
- "DAMP" DECID. FOREST

0   3   6 km

N

C

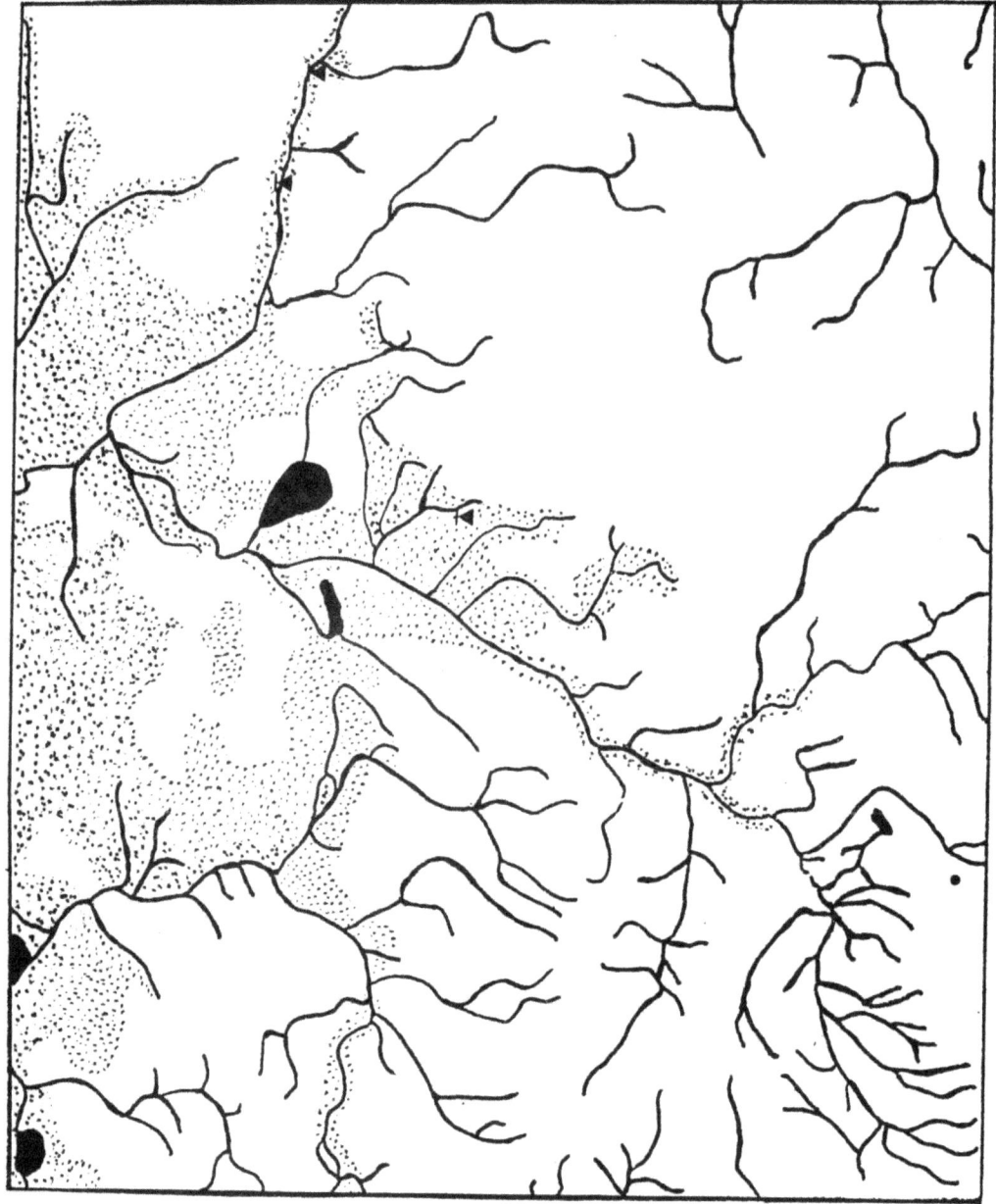

Map D: Late glacial settlement sites and surface finds in the Cambridge region.

BARBED POINT

SETTLEMENT LOCALE

0   3   6 km

D

Map E: Tranchet axe distribution in the Cambridge region.

E

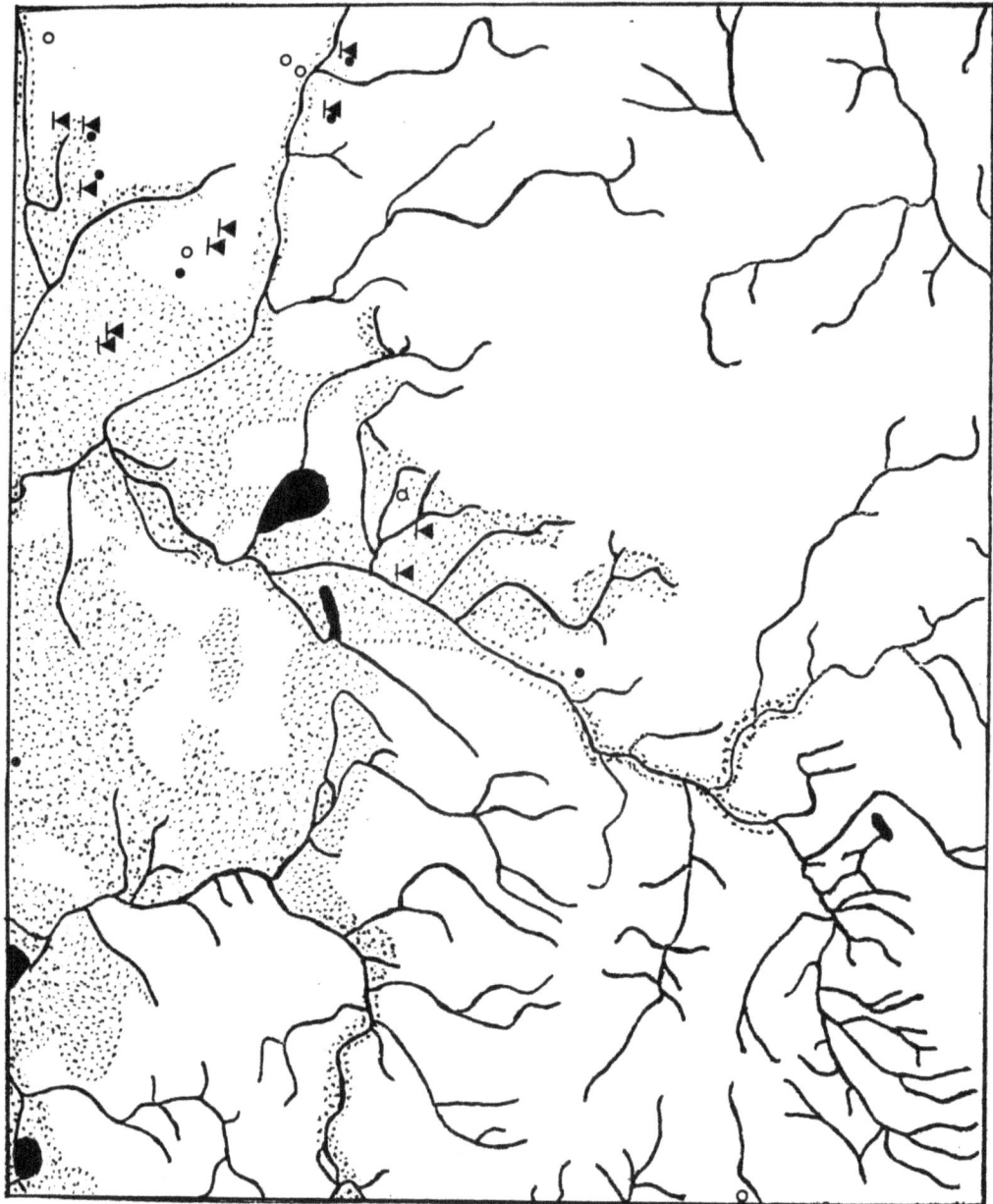

Map F: The distribution of Mesolithic sites in the Cambridge region.

F

N

● EARLY
○ INDETERMINATE
▲ LATE

0   3   6 km

Map G: Isolated surface finds in the Cambridge region (8,500–3,500 b.c.).

MICROLITHS

PEBBLE
MACEHEADS

N

0   3   6 km

G

Map H: The distribution of Neolithic axes in the Cambridge region.

POLISHED
FLINT AXES

● 5 – 10

• 1 – 5

GROUNDSTONE AXES

▲ 5 – 10

○ 1 – 5

0   3   6 km

H

Map J: The distribution of Neolithic projectile points in the Cambridge region.

LAUREL LEAF POINTS

14+

1–5

LEAF ARROWHEADS

50+

1–5

N

0   3   6 km

K

Map K: The distribution of Neolithic sites in the Cambridge region (for inset see Map L).

Map L: The distribution of Neolithic sites in the South-West of the Cambridge region in relation to soil types.

CHALK

ALLUVIUM

GAULT

TERRACE
GRAVELS

M II SURVEY
SITES

2 km.

N